Water Magic

*Harnessing the Power of the Natural Force
Found in the Ocean and Sea and the Secrets
of Celtic Witchcraft and Scottish Magick*

Your Free Gift (only available for a limited time)

Thanks for getting this book! If you want to learn more about various spirituality topics, then join Mari Silva's community and get a free guided meditation MP3 for awakening your third eye. This guided meditation mp3 is designed to open and strengthen ones third eye so you can experience a higher state of consciousness. Simply visit the link below the image to get started.

https://spiritualityspot.com/meditation

Contents

Introduction

So, you want to practice water magic? Well, you certainly picked the right book. Far too many people take the element of water for granted. Still, when you choose to work with its deep, mystical magic, you will unlock a level of power that will knock your socks off.

Water gives life. It, quite literally, shapes our world. It's in your blood, sweat, and tears. It governs your emotions and is also in your memories. This magical element retains information and can transmit intention and messages as well. Take a moment to imagine a world without water, and you'll quickly realize that that would be a world devoid of life and meaning.

Water is an element that refreshes and sustains us in so many ways. It's one of the major reasons we have nourishing food to eat – and it also feeds our souls. It can help transform you into the grandest version of yourself *if you just let it.* This strong, cleansing element is in you and all around you as well, and once you have the know-how, you can make it work for you in your magical practices, from rituals and spells to baths and washes.

In this book, you'll learn how to work directly with water and its symbols to design your life the way you want. You'll learn about the wisdom and rich history that flows through rivers, oceans, and all other bodies of water. You'll also discover the various manifestations of water in lore and mythology and get to know the magnificent goddesses and gods who wield the power of water.

Within these pages, you will learn how to practically apply water magic and the many spells and secrets associated with this element. Unlike other books on water magic, this one is incredibly easy to read and understand. You will find hands-on instructions and methods for your water magic practice and rituals and spells that are very easy to replicate. Don't be deceived by how easy it all seems, though, because the spells in this book will give you very tangible results when done right. To echo the often-repeated warning when it comes to magic and power: "Be careful what you wish for."

If you're an absolute novice to the world of magic, don't be nervous. This book will take you by the hand and walk you through everything you need to know to begin your water magic explorations. If you're an old hand at magic, you'll find knowledge in these pages that will prove invaluable to your practice and take your results to the next level.

If you're completely new to working with water and aren't entirely sure you'll get results, work with the same frame of mind as you would when performing other kinds of magic. Water magic will give you results, especially when you choose to work it with an open mind. In other words, it all comes down to intention. Keeping your desires clear and your mind free from self-doubt will boost the speed and efficacy of your practice. Keep that in mind, and you'll do just fine.

Chapter One: What Is Water Magic?

There are five major elements responsible for all life, and water is undoubtedly one of the most significant. Water magic is the process of working magic centered on the element of water. It doesn't matter whether you're working with just a drop of dew or the entire ocean. Water, within the realm of magic, can be used to manifest your desires and to boost your spiritual development as well.

The History of Water Magic

No one can survive without water forever. Even those who go on dry fasts for five days to a week know that they dare not push their bodies any further, or it's over for them. We've always needed freshwater as humans, not just to survive but to thrive as well. We've always sought out places with water to settle down and build entire civilizations around.

Water plays a significant part in the various creation stories and myths from cultures around the world. They all suggest that all things came from water. Even the theory of evolution supports that idea. So, let's get into the history of water magic and the various religions and cultures that work with water in supernatural ways.

Ancient Sumeria has a myth as old as about 3,000 BCE that speaks of the goddess who embodies the primal oceans. Her name is Nammu, and she is the mother of heaven and earth. From ancient Mesopotamia's creation myth — the Enuma Elish — we learn how the goddesses, gods, and earth were born. It is not precisely dated, but it's believed that the text is as old as the 9th century BCE, at least. We learn that the world began as nothing but freshwater and saltwater - bitter water in this text. Apsu represented freshwater, while Tiamat represented salty or bitter water. These waters go their separate ways only to join each other again to form the land and life as we know it.

Hindus have a creation hymn from the Rig Veda that talks about water as the beginning of all things. They also use water to cleanse and bless the faithful.

Muslims believe that all life comes from water. The Quran speaks of blessed rain falling upon the earth to water the crops and indicates that water represents the power and might of Allah. The indigenous American Iroquois people hold that all humans once lived in the sky, as there was no land. Then one day, a chief's daughter fell ill, and no one knew how to make well. Eventually, an elder told them they would find the solution by digging up the roots of a certain sacred tree. So, the people of that community dug and dug, creating a big hole. When they had done this, the chief's daughter and the tree fell down the hole.

In the hole was a large sea with just two swans. When both the tree and girl landed on the water, this caused a loud thunderclap that drew the swans' attention. They did their best to work out how to save the poor, frightened girl, but they couldn't figure out the best way to do that. So, they decided to ask the great turtle, who was the wisest of all creatures. The turtle told them that any gift that fell from above was a good omen, and he told them that they had to find the tree. They needed to find it with its roots as well as the soil that was attached to them. He said that this soil could be used to create an island for the girl to live on. So, the creatures began their search, and a toad finally found the tree in the ocean's depths. The toad took a mouthful of the dirt and resurfaced, then she spat out the soil and died. Then the soil, being magical, began to spread, and it soon became a very large piece of land which the girl could live on.

The land had no light, but the great turtle knew what to do about this as well. He told all digging animals to create holes in the sky to shine through and onto the newly formed landmass. Then, the girl became the mother of all in the new land. Another version of this myth claims that she got pregnant when she fell from the sky to the waters below.

The Quechan or **Yuma** is also indigenous North Americans. They believe that there was nothing but water and darkness in the beginning. It was rough, choppy water that formed a foam. This foam reached up and out and formed the sky. From the water came Bakotahl and Kokomaht, twin spirits who were collectively known as the Creator. Kokomaht was good, while Bakotahl was evil. As they both came up to the water's surface, Kokomaht had his eyes shut the entire time. Bakotahl had called out to his twin to see if his eyes were shut or open as they both surfaced. Because Kokomaht knew his brother was no good, he lied and claimed his eyes were open. So Bakotahl opened his eyes as they surfaced, and this blinded him. That's how he got his name, which means "the blind one."

Then both twins made the sacred directions. Kokomaht stepped out to the north, south, east, and west in four steps. After this, Bakotahl began making humans out of clay, but the humans had no fingers or feet. Kokomaht had a good laugh before deciding he would take over this job from Bakotahl, and that was how he made the perfect man and woman. This enraged Bakotahl, who then sent forth storms. In response, Kokomaht also became quite livid, and he stomped his feet hard. Some versions of this myth claim that the stomping caused an earthquake, casting all of Bakotahl's creations into the oceans, where they became waterfowl. Others say the stomping simply ended the storms. In both versions, these storms had left disease and sickness in their wake. With time, Kokomaht's people multiplied and took over the land, forming all the world's tribes. However, all wasn't well. There was now a frog in this world that grew to hate Kokomaht. Being very jealous of the god, he plotted to end him. The frog dug the ground out around Kokomaht's feet, causing him to sink. As Kokomaht went down, the frog took his breath away. Kokomaht didn't die in vain, as he taught his people about how death transforms one and all in the process.

In **Benin, Nigeria,** it's understood that all life came from water. This is a sentiment echoed by other cultures and traditions across West Africa. According to the Yoruba tribe of Nigeria, the world began as nothing but water. It had no form and no land. Olorun, the Supreme Being, dwelled above this formless water in the sky. He reached out to Orisha Nla, asking them to help him create the earth.

Nla started with a pigeon, a hen, and a snail shell filled with soil. He put the soil on a little patch and set the birds down. The birds scratched at the soil, scattering it about with their feet until there was both sea and land. When they were done, the Chameleon inspected their work and then gave Olorun a progress report, letting him know that Nla had done well. The very first place that had been created was called Ile Ife.

Christianity has water in its creation story as well. The Bible says, "In the beginning, God created the heaven and the earth. And the earth was without form, and void; and darkness was upon the face of the deep. And the Spirit of God moved upon the face of the waters." (Genesis Chapter 1, verses 1 to 2).

The world was nothing but water until God created light on the first day, and then a "firmament" to separate the waters so that they were both above and below. Then he created the land, plants, and other things.

The **Egyptian Pyramid Texts** talk about how the Creator God, Khepera, brought the world out of the waters of Nu. Nu represents all of the primeval matter from which all life springs. The water is more of a metaphor here, representing the invisible substance that makes up everything. Nut is Nu's female counterpart - a representation of the sky. According to ancient Egyptian mythology, the sky is another form of "water" in which all the heavenly bodies swim.

Water, Science, and the Occult

Scientific theories like the theory of evolution allude to life beginning in water. It's believed that tide pools and hot springs could be the possible spots where life began on earth. One theory states that about 600 million years ago, life began close to a hypothermal vent in the deep sea. This vent allowed life and various chemical reactions to thrive. The theory states that the life forms then moved to land about 500 million years ago.

Your body has a hundred times more water molecules than all the other molecules combined. Water is the one substance that can take the form of gas, liquid, and solid. It's great for functions like stabilization, reaction, transportation, communication, dilution, and lubrication. It's a good medium for connecting and sustaining all life. When you look at the chemical composition of water (two hydrogen atoms and one oxygen atom creating the molecule H_2O), you'll find that the molecules resemble tetrahedrons. The tetrahedron is a triangle with three dimensions and four faces. The oxygen atom rests right in the heart of this shape, while the hydrogen atoms face two of the four corners. The negatively charged oxygen of a water molecule is attracted to another molecule's positively charged atom, which creates the hydrogen bond between two or more molecules. The "scientific magic" of water lies in how these molecules interact with one another.

Consider this: water as ice will float on its liquid form, and that's why when a water pipe freezes, it bursts — the complete opposite of most other simple substances such as mercury, which would not produce the same reaction. Water can absorb lots of heat without its temperature rising, and that's why it's a great coolant. When water becomes steam as it boils, you have to pause and wonder, what exactly is vapor? What you think you see isn't the vapor itself but very little droplets of water as *liquid*.

Again, what is vapor? Where does it go? While science will tell you it's now in a gaseous state, occult science has a clearer, more honest answer. It has moved from the plane of the objective to that of the subjective. Science only acknowledges the gaseous, liquid, and solid as the three states of matter. However, occult science is aware of seven states, with four made of aether in varying degrees. In occult science, we know that the higher the state of a thing, the more freedom its molecules have to move.

Science is partially aware of this but hasn't yet fully grasped the implications. Chemists are aware that with solid water, each molecule usually has four hydrogen bonds around it. In liquid form, about 10 percent of those bonds are broken. It's now believed that water can take on a new structure as ice melts, where one molecule only latches on to two others close to it. When the water is at room temperature, only 80 percent of the molecules remain in this state. In contrast, the others have their usual four hydrogen bonds.

This difference implies that water mostly consists of chains that connect to one another rather than the seemingly solid tetrahedrons we once considered them to be. This distinction leads one to ponder the ability of water to form clusters or groups of molecules in a very different way from, say, regular tap water. The reason this happens is that water is intelligent. It can respond to any force that acts on it, including your intention... and that's why water magic works.

The Magical Properties of Water

Water's properties vary from one magic system to another and from person to person. It represents emotions, dreams, divination, destruction, restoration, purification, the underworld, the subconscious, transformation, and death. Water also represents intuition, friendship, harmony, rebirth, connection to ancestors, the spirit realm, the dead, and renewal. Its corresponding cardinal direction is West. In substance, water includes the ocean, tsunamis, creeks, rivers, lakes, ponds, waterfalls, rain, and more. The water Zodiac signs are Scorpio, Pisces, and Cancer. In astrology, water corresponds with Venus, Neptune, and the Moon. Magical tools of this element include the scrying mirror, bowl, chalice, and cauldron.

Animals connected to water include fish, whales, sharks, crabs, dolphins, seahorses, starfish, seals, otters, polar bears, penguins, walrus, squid, octopus, frogs, barracuda, seabirds, seagulls, and sea turtles. Magical creatures include the Chinese dragon, selkie, undine, kelpie, mermaid, sea serpent, and siren. The following are plants magically associated with water: blue lotus, belladonna, lobelia, burdock, lettuce, watermelon, periwinkle, seaweed, fern, algae, and aloe vera, bladderwrack, Irish moss, Atlantic kelp, agar, and the water lily. Here are the other correspondences of water:

Court Cards: Queens

Organs: Bladder, kidney.

Qualities: Moist, heavy, cold, deep, dissolving, reflecting, ripping, fluid, abysmal, resurging, solid, obscure, motioned.

Stones: Lapis lazuli, loliote, fluorite, moonstone, blue agate, lepidolite, beryl, aquamarine, emerald, pearl, jade, opal, jade, larimar, blue crystal, and all kinds of shells.

Metal: Silver

Colors: Blue, green, aqua, teal, indigo, turquoise, cream, white, silver, seafoam green.

Tarot Trump: The Moon, The Lovers, The Hanged Man, Death

Tibetan Wisdom: Reflection

Rune: Laguz

Tibetan Failing: Hatred

Taste: Salty

Time of Year: Winter

Time of Day: Dusk

Best Times to Practice Water Magic: Between 9 AM to 12 PM and 9 PM to 12 AM.

Day: Monday, and any day with a Full Moon.

Kinds of Magic: Mirror magic, scrying, psychic work, relationship magic, purification, cleansing, healing, blessing, dream magic, curses, moon magic, and weather magic.

If you've never worked with water before in your magic rituals, you're in for a pleasant surprise. The power of this element is often underestimated. I assure you that your connection to the magical world will be radically transformed in ways you never deemed possible. Little wonder, since water is an element that leads to lasting transformation. It blesses you, restores you, and refreshes you, and it does the same for your magic, too. Learning the ways of water will leave you wondering why you've waited so long to work with this element.

There's no better way to work with water than to get to know the spirits, gods, and goddesses that rule this element. As you learn about their mythology, how they're connected to water, and what aspects of water they represent, you will be able to decide how to go about your rituals. The key to practicing magic, regardless of its form, is to personalize it. So, through these stories, you can consider the properties of water and how they affect you. There's also the added bonus of personalizing water and its various aspects by working with these sacred, powerful beings. This way, you feel like your craft is authentic and comes from a place of truth.

Chapter Two: Water Entities — Mermaids, Elementals, and Naiads

There are many mythological beasts and deities with extremely powerful ties to water. The mythology of these beings has been passed down from generation to generation to teach people to respect the water, care for it, and be aware of its power and danger. Let's talk about some of these creatures in this chapter.

Nereids are creatures that represent the beauty and kindness of the sea. These creatures have melodious voices and are usually depicted as beautiful girls with red coral branches as crowns, barefoot with gold-trimmed, white robes made of silk. They went around with Poseidon, carrying his trident for him. The most popular of them are Poseidon's wife Amphitrite (also Triton's mother), Thetis (Achilles' mother), Psamanthe (mother of Phocus), and Galatea (who the Cyclops Polyphemus was interested in romantically). In total, Doris and Nereus have 50 daughters. They are also depicted riding dolphins and other sea creatures. They represent the journeys we undertake in death and marriage.

Naiads are also nymphs in Greek mythology. They are female spirits who rule over wells, fountains, streams, springs, brooks, and bodies of fresh water. Not to be mistaken for river gods who are the embodiments of rivers, naiads were central to the local cults of ancient times and were worshipped heavily. It was tradition for girls and boys to offer locks of their hair at the local springs to the naiads at their coming-of-age festivities. In Lerna, the naiads were sought out with water rituals to cleanse the people. These cleansings were both magical and medicinal. Oracles could also be found and consulted right by the ancient springs.

Naiads can be as dangerous as they are benevolent. For instance, there is the tale of Hylas, a youth who was a servant and companion to Heracles. He was aboard the *Argo* when the naiads spotted him. They became enthralled with his beauty, and so they kidnapped him. These creatures are also rather jealous. The Sicilian poet Theocritus talks about the story of a shepherd named Daphnis, who had been in love with an Arcadian nymph named Nomia or Echenais. Several times, Daphnis had been unfaithful to her. As revenge, she chose to blind him permanently.

There's also the tale of Hermaphroditus, born of Hermes and Aphrodite. He was such a handsome boy that Salmacis was smitten by him. She actually tried to rape him and sought to be united with him for always. She prayed for this, and her prayer was answered by a god quite literally: he fused both their bodies together to become one person, a hermaphrodite. You'll notice that the name is a fusion of the names Aphrodite and Hermes. When this fusion occurred, her spring gained the ability to make the men who bathed in it effeminate and soft.

Merfolk have existed for thousands and thousands of years, showing up across mythos and stories from Africa, Asia, Europe, Indonesia, New Zealand, Australia, and the Americas. The earliest record of these water people is on Oannes of the ancient Babylonians, around 200 BCE. He had the body of a fish, but his feet and head were of a man. It is said that he reached out to humanity and gave us powerful knowledge. He showed people how to create living spaces and gather food and other resources. Legend has it that each night, he would retreat to the sea to sleep.

The Syrian sea and moon goddess called Atargatis was also a mermaid who took off to the sea for her own safety after killing her mortal lover. She took on the form of a woman with a fishtail, and that's how she became a mermaid goddess. In medieval times, there was no question in anyone's mind that the waters of the sea had mermaids in them. You can find them depicted in literature and art all around the world.

From what we know of mermaids, they have the head and body of a woman with a fish's tail. Middle English referred to the sea or lake as mere, so these creatures are the "maids of the sea." They come in all forms. Some of them have scaly tails, while others are smooth, and others still have no tail. They can walk on land if they want to by switching to human legs. Contact with water makes them revert to their true form, so they avoid it unless they're ready to head back. Aside from mermaids, mermen, merbabies, and merchildren also exist. They're collectively referred to as merfolk.

Most of these creatures' stories involve revenge, betrayal, woe, and suffering, with barely any happy endings. There's the tale of Alexander the Great discovering the fountain of youth and immortality. He took a flask, filled it with this water, and then went home. He used this water to wash his sister's hair. When he hit age 32, he fell ill and died. His sister, Thessalonike, was overcome with grief. She tried to kill herself by drowning in the sea, but because her brother had washed her hair with the water of immortality, she didn't die. She became a mermaid instead and dwelled in the Aegean for several hundred years. It's said that the whole time when she ran into a sailor, she would ask them if Alexander was still alive. If they answered, "He lives and reigns and conquers the world," she would allow them to go on their journey unharmed. If they gave any other answer, she would become a Gorgon similar to Medusa. Then she would cause everyone on the ship to die a watery death.

The mermaids you find close to the tropical coasts are the friendly ones. Light-hearted, they'll sing lovely songs and flirt with sailors. They love to decorate themselves with sea glass, pearls, and other shiny objects. The mermaids who dwell in the ocean's depths aren't friendly. They're spiteful, tough, and hard. They're the sort who will sink a ship simply because they're bored. Mermaids in Japan are more like fish in their looks and a lot smaller than usual. They enjoy challenging humans to skillful games where the price of losing is death. These mermaids feast on children and those who go swimming on their own close to their homes. For the most part, however, mermaids have kind hearts, can grant wishes, and also bring you good fortune.

Mermen aren't as common as mermaids because they don't have many dealings with humanity unless they've fallen in love with a human female. Traditionally, they protect and guard the merfolk fiercely. If anyone aboard a ship ever hurts a mermaid, you can rest assured they'll create a fierce storm and sink that ship in a rageful fit. The scariest group of mermen are the Blue Men of the Minch, who live off Scotland's coast in the Outer Hebrides. They're called the Blue Men because of their blue skin. They also have gray beards. According to the lore, before they besiege a ship, they first issue a challenge to its captain — a rhyming challenge, to be precise. If the captain is good with words and thinks on his feet fast enough to win this "oceanic rap battle," he can keep himself and his sailors safe.

Finfolk is from Orkney folklore. These beings are sorcerers with the ability to shapeshift. The Finman and Finwife are known for kidnapping unsuspecting youth who frolic close to the shore and fishermen, forcing them to spend their lives as their spouses and servants. The Finman is thin, tall, and has a gloomy, serious face. He has many magical abilities, such as being able to row between Orkney and Norway in just seven strokes of the oar. He's a crafty one, always ready to steal a man's wife or silver. He typically does his best to stay away from humans. Still, being territorial, he won't hesitate to destroy any boats that move along his waters. To keep him from doing this, sailors will draw a cross with tar or chalk on the bottom of their craft as the Finfolk absolutely can't stand the Christian symbol.

The Finwife begins life as a stunningly beautiful mermaid, with the single objective of getting a human husband. If she succeeds, she'll take the man to Finfolkaheem to live with her, or she could decide to live with him instead. If she fails, she has to marry a Finman and work ashore as a spinner or healer by him, forced to give him all her silver or risk being horribly beaten. She usually has a black cat and can become a fish to send messages to her family in Finfolkaheem.

In Australian folklore, the **bunyip** is a terrifying creature that dwells in riverbeds, creeks, swamps, and waterholes. This creature is as aggressive as it is hairy, and it has a taste for human flesh — even more so that of children and women. This beast has powerful magic and is considered the real source of all evil in the world.

Ashrays are Scottish creatures, and some refer to them as fair folk. These nocturnal, translucent beings can look like young women or men, mostly living beneath the water. If they're exposed to sunlight, they melt right away and become a puddle.

The Scandinavian **Fossie Grim** (or Fossiegrim) is a very handsome spirit of water. He draws people to their watery deaths by playing enchanting violin music. Some say that he can be very benevolent, blessing those he favors. The Fossie Grim beings love waterfalls, and they hold them as sacred. They look like youth with fair hair, and their feet become one with the foam formed at the bottom of a waterfall. They are also fantastic at playing the harp, so if you want to master this instrument, you could make offerings to them by the water.

Bäckahästen is a horse from Scandinavian and German lore. The word means "brook horse," so you can infer that they live in brooks. They also dwell in rivers and will lure in people who pass by.

The **hippocamp** is from Greek mythology. This massive, formidable sea being has a horse's head and the tail of a dolphin or fish, and Poseidon has a team of them pulling his chariot.

The **Loch Ness Monster** is one of the most infamous creatures of the sea. There have been thousands of sightings of this creature which dwells in Loch Ness, Scotland. Also called the Nessie, it's believed to be a prehistoric reptile or eel. There's also the **Chessie** of Chesapeake Bay in the US. This creature looks like a sea snake but with a hump on its back.

According to folktales from Britain, **Jenny Greenteeth** is a hag that dwells in the bottom of ponds and lakes. This hag drags unsuspecting kids down to watery graves. She's also sometimes depicted as a fairy. She's reminiscent of Peg Powler, an English water witch with green skin. It's said that you can find Greenteeth in lakes that have duckweed all over them. Some places refer to duckweed as Jenny Greenteeth as well.

Scylla is a mythical creature that dwells in Scylla, the narrow Messina strait between Sicily and Calabria. It's believed that on the other end of this strait is yet another beast called Charybdis. Scylla is Hecate's daughter, a water nymph poisoned by a rival out of jealousy in a sea pool. The poisoning left her looking gruesome.

The **Kraken** is from Norway and Iceland. It's a giant octopus that was first sighted as early as the 12th century. The word translates to "unhealthy animal," and rightfully so, as this creature is covered with spikes, tentacles, and suckers.

The **Kelpie** is a water horse. According to Celtic legend, they live close to streams, rivers, and freshwater lakes. They can shapeshift at will, using that ability to entrance and seduce humans. You can tell you're looking at a kelpie thanks to seaweed in their hair.

The **Rusalka** is from Slavic mythology. These water maidens resemble mermaids and sirens, and their singular objective is to drive people beneath the water to their death.

The **Lorelei** is a sea spirit. Also spelled Loreley, she is the queen or maiden of the Rhine. She could be treacherous or benevolent, just like the Rhine River itself.

Kappas are from Japanese myths. They are water vampires or goblins – about the same size as a nine-year old child - but with ridiculous strength! Some say that these terrifying beings resemble monkeys (somewhat) and occupy oceans, streams, rivers, and lakes. They attack horses and livestock by sucking the blood out of their anuses. It's important to be polite to these beings. Some say you should offer them a cucumber that has your name etched into it.

The **Leviathan** is an epic sea serpent that shows up in a Canaanite poem from Ugarit, in Mesopotamian myths, and more recently in the Old Testament of the Bible. It's depicted as a water dragon or serpent, although ancient Hungarian legends refer to it as a whale. Whatever its form, this beast is a dangerous one. Followers of the Kabbalah consider all stories of the Leviathan and its mate as representatives of Samael and Lilith.

Selkies are from Celtic myths. They live in caves underwater. These beings are kind and benevolent in their dealings with humans. According to legend, they are the manifestation of the souls of those who have drowned. Others say they are fallen angels who, while having fallen from grace in heaven, are too pure to be in hell. They love people deeply. To summon them, all you have to do is cry seven tear drops into the sea. When they're in love, they're happy to shed their seal skins and dwell on land with their lovers.

Sirens will sing the most intoxicating songs that lure people to their death or grant eternal life. In South and Central America, there is the well-known legend of La Llorona or the "Weeping Woman." From the waist up, this creature is strikingly beautiful. Those who hear her song cannot keep away. They feel compelled to go to her, and this is how they die.

The **Uncegila** is a horned water serpent with spots, shiny scales, and a crest that sparkles. It brings death and blindness.

The **Vodianoi** are green-bearded old men with slime, scales, and hair all over them. They dwell in sunken ships.

Deities

Many deities dwell in all kinds of water bodies and forms, including rivers, wells, lakes, oceans, and streams. As it relates to energy, these deities could be cold, hot, or anything in between. Some of them belong to particular places, while others aren't restricted to any particular area. The energy of water is distinctly feminine, so, understandably, there are lots of feminine deities, goddesses, and orishas associated with this element. Let's quickly run through the most common of them, so you can find the one(s) that you're drawn to the most.

Amphitrite is a Greek goddess who rules the ocean. Her home is an undersea cave. Aphrodite is considered the Greek goddess of desire and love and a counterpart to the Roman goddess Venus. She rules fertility, sensuality, pleasure, art, and beauty. When her father, Ouranos, was castrated, his penis fell into the sea, and the mixture of semen and blood gave birth to this goddess, who is the ultimate enchantress. A dove, her animal spirit, usually accompanies her.

Amberella is a Lithuanian goddess of the ocean. If you honor her, she will bless you with gifts from the sea. She can help you with money, fertility, and love problems.

Avnova is also called Abnoba, Abnova, Dea Abnoba, and Dianae Abnobae, among other names. She's in charge of Germany's sacred waters in the Black Forest. Her name comes from the word Avon, which means "river."

Anahita is the Persian goddess who rules fertility and the mysteries of femininity. She has a chariot with four horses, each representing clouds, wind, rain, and sleet. Connected to rivers, lakes, and all waters, she also rules over the waters of childbirth. She is connected to Aphrodite, Anat, Astarte, Ishtar, and Athena. Anahita means "the immaculate one."

Atahensic is also called Atanensic, Ata-en-sic, Aataentsic, Ataensiq, Sky Woman, and other names. She is from the Iroquois and Huron tribes of North America. Legend has it that she fell out of the sky through a hole, was saved by birds of the sea, placed on a turtle's back, and taken to Turtle Island, her present home. She is all about fertility, marriage, and female craftwork.

Boann is from Ireland, and she rules over the Boyne River. Also called the "White Cow," she once trespassed the water's boundaries and met a tragic death. The Boyne is close to the ancient, sacred tombs of Dowth, Knowth, and Newgrange, and it's a river full of mystery and power. Boyne, the goddess, had broken one of the sacred well's taboos by looking into the holy water. She is the patron of creativity, poetry, knowledge, fertility, and divine inspiration.

Berba is one of the three sisters in charge of Southeast Ireland's rivers. She is the lady of the Barrow River.

Bai Tanki is an interesting goddess from India. Her tragic story is pretty extreme. As a young woman, many men found her desirable, so much so they tried to rape her. She resorted to magic to save herself from them, and that's how sexually transmitted diseases came to be. When each man would try to overpower and assault her, his penis would instantly be afflicted with a disease. Despite her efforts, one of the men eventually had his way with her, causing her much sorrow and pain. As a result, she became a river and spread those diseases all around the earth. She's the goddess that is usually invoked when practicing revenge magic, especially for women who a man has wronged in any way.

Brigit, the fiery one, is of Celtic roots. She is connected to the sacred flame and to springs and healing water. She is the patron deity of poets, sailors, midwives, fugitives, hearth, and prophecy. She also protects many animals, including owls, snakes, bees, lambs, and cows.

Coventina is a goddess from Rome who is in charge of the ancient, holy spring near Britain's Hadrian's Wall. She is depicted as a water nymph with a beaker or jug in her hands.

Chalchihuitlicue is a goddess even older than the Aztec civilization of ancient Mexico. She's sensual and young and rules over all water that flows. She can cause destruction by flood or give life with her living waters. Her name means "lady of the green skirt," which explains her association with the stone jade. You can find her wearing colors like blue and green, with water lilies in her hair. She has a blue nose ring that has snakes on each end. It's believed that she causes great whirlpools and rains and spares those she favors by turning them into fish so they can live. She's also connected to snakes and is considered the protector of fishermen and kids.

Idemili presides over the Idemili River in Anambra, an Igbo state in Eastern Nigeria. She gives her protection to mothers, women in childbirth, and infants. She loves and defends them fiercely. Idemili shares a deep bond with snakes — especially the python. Her river is full of them, and there are a host of shrines dedicated to her worship. She's the one to turn to when you want peace, progress, reversal of curses, favor with one and all, and blessings all around.

Isis is both a queen and a goddess originally worshipped in Egypt by the Nile River Valley. She is the epitome of the divine feminine and maternal energy. She is all about healing, fertility, the moon's power, marriage, abundance, love, beauty, and the mysteries of life after death. Also called Usert, Ast, Aset, and Eset, among other names, some of her gemstones are lapis lazuli, emerald, coral, amethyst, moonstone, bloodstone, turquoise, and ruby. Cats, lions, cows, scorpions, and the sphinx are sacred creatures to her. The ankh is her symbol, and it resembles the bloodstone amulets made for her, called the "Isis knot."

Ganga rules over the River Ganges. This Hindu goddess has half herself in the river, while her other half dwells in the Milky Way. She has the power to wash away all your karma from your present and past lives as well. Turn to her if you need healing, purification, and energy for your soul and body.

Jurate rules over the mermaids according to Lithuanian folktales. She's always crying, but her tears are far from ordinary. Those tears are pure amber. She is the ultimate healing force.

Julinggul is from Australia. This goddess, a serpent colored like the rainbow, represents seawater and rainwater. She can show up as a lightning storm and is a prominent feature in Australian creation myths.

Juturna is the Roman goddess of rivers, wells, fountains, and springs. January 11 is the Juturnalia which is when she is celebrated. She shows up in the works of Ovid, Virgil, and other writers of the classical era. She is associated with healing and immortality, both of which she grants her faithful followers through her sacred waters.

Kymopoleia is part of the Greek pantheon. Also called Cymopoleia, this nymph dwells in the sea and is married to Briareos, a storm giant. She is in charge of the storm's fierce waves.

The **Korrigans** are dangerous deities who draw in their victims by dancing every night and then drowning them. They show up in Celtic lore.

Keto is also called Ceto. She rules over the monsters of the sea.

Mami Wata is not like the other goddesses who are often restricted to just one location or one sacred body of water. This African deity represents water in every form. If there's water where you are, then she is there in her fullest, most radiant form. She is often depicted as a mermaid with two tails. She is considered an Iwa or Orisa of water. While Oshun the Orisa is the river's Ashe, Mami Wata's sacred energy is connected to rivers and all forms of water. Mami Wata is honored in Benin. Many groups there pledge allegiance to her, and their connection with the water is deep. They are incredible mediums as well.

The **Morrigan** are goddesses of the river in Ireland. They are connected specifically with the River Unius. Sometimes, they are portrayed as just one goddess, while at other times as a trinity. Morrigan translates to "great phantom queen." She is a warrior who wields magic as her weapon. She shares a connection with the Lamia, who are demons of the night associated with Lilith, the goddess of old. The Morrigan has the crow as her totem, and she rules over mystery, death, and magic.

Miriam is an incredible prophetess who was mentioned in the Bible. The sister of Moses, she is in charge of the women who dance at the sea of reeds. Miriam is beloved by many feminists who worship her on Saturday nights. According to legend, Miriam was followed by a well of water as she went through the wilderness. With this water, many had their thirst quenched and grew healing herbs.

Oba is the Orisa of the Oba River in Osun and Oyo States in Western Nigeria, the land of the Yoruba tribes. She is also part of the religion and pantheon of the La Regla Lucumi. A wife to the Yoruba god of thunder, Sango, Oba had once cut off her ears to feed them to her husband, an act that bred mistrust and sadness between the couple.

Osun is the river Orisa in charge of the money, marriage, gold, dance, beauty, and other wonderful things. She is often represented by artistic depictions of Our Lady of Copper, Caridad del Cobre, whose feast day is September 8. Osun's colors are gold and yellow, and her altars are elaborately decorated. According to legend, she had once been short on cash, and things were difficult for her, despite being a queen. As a result, she went to the river each day to hand wash her clothes. With time, the river turned her clothes yellow, and consequently, that became her color. The Osun River is a recognized UNESCO World Heritage site. This goddess is all about appreciating joy and creativity.

Yemoja is also called Yemaya. She is also from Yoruba land and was honored on September 7. She is worshipped by those who follow the ways of Santeria (La Regla Lucumi), Ifa, Candomble, and the Voodoo practice of New Orleans. She is usually offered seaweed, spearmint, basil, gardenia, eucalyptus, lotus, lemon balm, and myrrh. Black molasses, pineapple, whole watermelon, fish, and coconut are sacred to her, among others. Her sacred energy, or Ashe, is the ocean. Wherever you have water from the ocean, she's there. Her colors are white and blue, just like the sea. She is the mother, kind, gentle, nurturing, and fierce when those she calls her own are wronged or hurt.

Chapter Three: Water Witches of the Seas, Lakes, and Beyond

There are all sorts of water witches. You should be aware of them to know what kind of magical path you are drawn to. However, it's fine to feel as though you resonate with more than one sort of water witchcraft, so you should never feel confined to just one. In the end, magic is a personal practice. You may start with general knowledge, but with time, you will make it your own.

Well Witches

This kind of witch interacts with wells. Most folklores have always alluded to wells as being the sacred spaces of the Fae and other magical creatures. Wells can also be doorways to other worlds besides this one, and most of them have magical powers such as healing and making one's wishes come true.

Some wells are more famous than others. For instance, a well belonging to the goddess Coventina of Romano-British origin was discovered by John Clayton, a British archeologist, and excavated in 1876. In this well were dedications to the goddess that had been in a walled-off part meant to contain a spring's outflow. It's now called Covetina's Well. Besides dedication slabs, there were 13 487 coins,

10 altars dedicated to Minerva and Coventina, the statue of a man's head, votive offerings, 2 clay incense burners, and the carvings of 3 water nymphs in the well.

There's also the Madron Well, in Madron, Cornwell, which is in the United Kingdom. It's a Cornish Celtic holy spring at ground level with healing powers. There's an account of a poor cripple called Jon Trelile who had been cured by the waters of this spring when he had a bath in them and then slept on a grassy hillock; this was before 1641. Every year, the mound has been redone, and it's been named Saint Maderne's Bed.

On May Day at the Madron Well, young people would perform a ceremony to learn how long they'd have to wait to get married. The ceremony involved taking two grass or straw stems about an inch long and connecting them with a pin. The youth would then let the fastened grass drop into the water and count how many bubbles would rise after. For each bubble that came up, it would represent a year before they could be wed. Eventually, the ceremony was moved to Sundays rather than May Day – as the youth had to work on weekdays.

If you'd like to be a well water witch, you should look up well deities like Brigid, Fontus, and Saint Hilda. It would be helpful is you have access to well water too.

In all your magical acts, you should be respectful. Never take from the water without asking the permission of your preferred deity or deities, and always thank them for being so generous.

River Witches

Much of the folklore surrounding river water holds that spirits can't cross rivers. So, rivers are a barrier between the physical and spiritual world. It's not hard to figure out why rivers have always been considered sacred. It's also believed that water is connected to direction, and water that flows toward the sun offers healing power.

If you find that you have a connection with river water, you should take the time to get used to the watercourses around you. Become familiar with the spirits and deities who dwell in rivers by consciously reaching out to them. A straightforward way to do this is simply to sit by the banks, silent and expectant. You could also honor these beings by cleaning the place, picking up any litter in or around the water, showing them that you do honor them and want to connect with them.

To be a true river magician, you should look within to find which deity or beings you resonate with the most. Establishing a connection with them will greatly amplify the results of your water magic. You can look into Danau, Boanne, and the Welsh nymph Sabrina, among others. When collecting water from the river, seek permission. Express your gratitude to the water and those who preside over it.

Marsh, Bog, and Swamp Witches

Unfortunately, there are too many negative depictions of marsh and swamp witches all through history. The truth is that, like with all things in life, these can be good or evil. If you are drawn to this path, it might mean that you love to work with both the dark and light aspects of magic. It might also mean that you're a non-conformist who doesn't care for the expectations and traditions adhered to by society.

While Hollywood makes marsh, bog, and swamp witches seem to be all about darkness and hopelessness, the truth is that marshes and swamps are incredibly fertile. The witch who chooses this path will naturally mix the elements of plant or green witchcraft with water. If this applies to you, you should be respectful in collecting plants and water for your magical practice.

You might want to work with the swamp dew that's found on bog plants in the evenings. These drops of dew are magic and can help with beauty and healing. If you want to store the dew, then you must get up before dawn so that the sun's heat doesn't cause the moisture to evaporate. You can store them in vials with secure toppers and keep them somewhere cool.

If this is the water witchcraft path that calls to you, then you might want to check out the Matronae Aufinae. These goddesses are Germanic in origin and were worshipped fervently in the part of Rhineland that the Roman Empire oversaw. It is believed that their name translates to "Goddesses of the Swampy Place."

Lake Witches

The waters of the lake may be still, but as the saying goes, "still waters run deep." The lake witches are among some of the most peaceful and calm ones. They are usually tranquil people who value peace above all else. If this sounds like you, you could test that theory by going for a dip in your local lakes or walking around the circumference. You can take in the fauna and flora that thrive there and see how you feel about them.

In the interest of full disclosure, it should be mentioned that ghosts are drawn to lakes because the water acts as a great conductor for energy – and ghosts *like that*. Ghosts can draw energy from all kinds of places, and the still waters of the lake give them all the energy they need to manifest and move around. For instance, the Lady of the Lake resides in Texas, at White Rock Lake; check it out at **https://whiterocklake.org/white-rock-lake/lady-of-the-lake/**. The Fossegrim are spirits of water who love to lure people to watery graves in lakes by playing sweet violin music. The Japanese Kappas will drag kids beneath the water to drink their blood.

The point is, there are lots of legends of lakes being haunted, but you should by no means let this stop you from working with them if you feel naturally drawn to them. Just make sure to seek their permission to use the lake water, and always express genuine gratitude as you do so. An interesting deity to look into is the Celtic goddess Cerridwen, a lady of the lake and a witch you can invoke when you cast a spell or perform a ritual. You can also work with the Lake Maidens called the Gwragedd Annwn, from Welsh lore.

Sea Witches

If you're a sea witch, you'll know it. You'll feel it in your bones when you're at the beach. The sea witch works with the elements of the ocean, including the moon. They work with seashells, sand, and seawater. They're often depicted as a woman trekking along the shores who has curios and charms made of ocean flotsam. It's believed that the sea witch can create storms out of nothing and cause ships to sink.

European folklore has featured the sea witch for many centuries. They would show up among those who worked with the sea as sailors or fishermen. They might present as a fairy, selkie, or mermaid, or they could be regular humans who know how to work the sea's magic to bring about their desired results.

Sea witches can control the weather and wind, help or hinder the fisherman at work, and harness the power of the moon and the tides it causes. When a sea witch is offended, it could spell major trouble. Ancient lore has it that when sailors went on voyages, they would have a rope tied with three knots. The witches had told them that pulling on the first knot would give them a southeasterly wind, gentle in nature. Pulling the second one would bring a northerly wind, nice and strong. The third knot would cause a hurricane. Some lore had it that the witches could conjure up lost treasure from shipwrecks, or when asked, return the body of a drowned child, lover, or husband so that they could be properly buried. To do this, one would have to throw a ring or a coin into the sea to pay the witch.

One of the more popular witches is Calypso, who enchanted Odysseus' ship to lure it to her island. At the same time, she made all ships that attempted to follow to rescue him unable to come along. She also had the power to keep the weather on her island perpetually lovely so that Odysseus would want nothing more than to stay right where he was.

Sea witches are drawn to the moon's power and work with the ocean's tides and the moon's phases. They'll collect beach sand, shells, sea glass, crab claws, cockles, driftwood, clam, cowries, stones, and seawater as well. Each element has its special energy and use. You can learn each one and figure out the tide tables of your local sea. If you feel like this resonates with you, you should go to the beach often and allow its energy to feed you with wisdom, strength, and blessings.

Have you always loved the sound of the waves crashing on the shore? Do you relish the feel of the powerful breeze on your skin? How about the feel of sand in between your toes? Or how the ground seems to suck you in as you trudge along the beach? In that case, you really should consider working sea magic.

The first thing to do is become intimate with the sea by deliberately connecting with it. You've got to visit it regularly, learn all you can about it, and spend time with it. You could also collect things you find on the shore that speak to you and take them home with you. Use them to decorate your space, and they will draw the power of the sea into your home.

Consider creating an altar to the sea or your preferred sea deity. You can work with the four elements if you like, bringing something to represent Earth, air, fire, and of course, water. Incense can stand in for air, and a candle's flame will work fine for fire. For Earth, you can use salt or sand from the beach and use the seawater for water. For your incense, consider working with herbs that grow by the sea naturally, like rosemary, sage, basil, and lavender.

Another great practice is to give offerings to the sea spirits and deities. Your gift should be something of value to them, so do some research into what they like. If you can't find anything they like, you can give them things that matter to you. You could create simple jewelry or works of art by the shore or just collect flowers and throw them into the sea in thanksgiving and worship. You can also help clean up the beach and save sea animals who need help, signaling to the spirits that you're ready and willing to work with them. So, they will happily throw their power behind any water ritual you practice or spell you work. Don't just try to connect with them for what they can offer you, but for the joy of communion. In other words, you don't have to only go to them when you need something. Make it a regular practice, and watch how both your life and your magic blossom beautifully.

Kinds of Sea Magic

When it comes to sea magic, there are all sorts of ways to work with it. Sea magic can be further split into weather magic and beach magic. The materials are always connected to the sea, no matter the form you choose. You can work with the same spells you already do if you're a practicing witch. Still, the only difference between one form of sea magic and another would be the materials. For instance, rather than using regular salt, you could use sea salt instead. Also, the sheer number of shells you can find on the sea have their unique uses.

The thing about working with sea spirits is that they can be dangerous when you offend them. Still, this will hardly be a concern if your intention is not to start trouble, to begin with. Approach them with respect and reverence, and they will help you with whatever you need. All you must know to help you with your sea magic are the sea correspondences that matter. Here's a list to help you:

Metal: Silver

Gems: Moonstones, clear quartz, emeralds, coral, shells, pearls, and aquamarines.

Colors: White, black, blue, and emerald, green.

Tools: Cauldron, mirror, broom, cup, comb, bucket, and mop.

Symbols: Spiral, moon, crescent, wave, lightning bolt, and cloud.

Foods and Herbs: Seaweeds like nori and kelp, shellfish and fish, watermelon, bouillabaisse, cantaloupe, coconut, champagne, rosemary, honeydew melon, chamomile, parsley, spearmint, watercress, sea salt, basil, and white rum.

Note that if you want to work with the herbs by extracting their oils, you should only ever use them after mixing them with a good base or carrier oil like jojoba oil. If you don't, you run the risk of getting a burn or irritating your skin. You should also do a patch test on your skin by applying the oil to a small, unnoticeable part of your body and wait to see if there is an adverse reaction.

Beach magicians work with the ocean's tides, which are controlled by the moon. It helps to look up the tides before you begin working beach magic. There are tide tracking apps you can download for this. When the tide's coming in, it's known as **flow;** it is the best time to work magic relating to new beginnings, transformation, and change. **High tide** will happen twice a day at 12-hour intervals when the sea hits the beach's highest point, and it's the best time to work magic involving passion, strength, and courage. **Springtide** happens during the New Moon and Full Moon in each cycle of the moon. The Earth, Moon, and Sun line up to form a very high tide, and this can give your magic a powerful boost.

Ebb is when the tide's heading back out and is a good time for cleansing and banishing magic. The **low tide** comes around 6 hours after the High Tide is over. At this point, the sea is at the beach's lowest point, and you can find so many treasures at the sea line. This tide presents a suitable time for planning, introspection, and meditation magic.

Neap tides happen during the 1st and 3rd quarters of every lunar cycle. They happen because of the angle of the moon and the sun in relation to the Earth. The sun's gravity cancels out that of the moon, which leads to a very, very low tide that is not conducive to magical work. You won't get much in the way of results at this time.

Moon magic is part of sea magic, as the moon controls the sea. Just as it causes physical tides, it also causes etheric tides, which you can take advantage of for your rituals. Also, note that all spherical, round, or shiny objects are influenced by Luna (the moon). The best time to practice divination and scrying is when the moon is full, and it's even better when you're right beneath the moonlight.

Weather magic involves tinkering with nature, and that's no easy feat since nature is beautiful chaos. So, before you work this sort of magic, you need to study nature and align yourself with it. You need to observe the forces of nature and see how they work with one another.

While weather magic can allow you to change the course of the weather, you will find it's not an easy thing to do as it's just easier to go with Mother Nature's flow. Also, there are consequences for choosing to oppose nature. Just because you want to work a spell doesn't mean that the present moment is the perfect time to do so. You need to deeply consider whether the rituals you're about to work that go against the course of nature are actually worth it. You should work weather magic in line with the current weather. Trying to cause rainfall when it's not needed could lead to disasters, just as summoning the sun in a storm could be horrible in the long run.

Chapter Four: Creating Your Water Magic Altar

If you're lucky, you live close to a body of water that you can use as a sacred space to practice water magic and rituals. Even if you don't, it's still a good idea to have a water altar, indoors or outdoors. This way, you can have access to the power of the element whenever you want. You might not be able to go to wonderful, holy water sites like Snoqualmie Falls, Niagara Falls, Lake Pontchartrain, or Lake Manasarovar, all with their unique energy and power. However, you can still create your own shrine or altar where water magic will work just as powerfully.

All Elements Matter

The thing about creating a water shrine is that you'll need to add items that represent each of the five elements. The reason for this is that you want to make sure there's balance as you work your rituals. The other elements are just as vital as water in helping you get the most bang for your buck.

Earth

To represent the element of earth, you could use a crystal associated with water. Crystals are naturally of the earth, but that doesn't mean that's the only element they're associated with. Some crystals are reminiscent of water, while others were created in the water. Turquoise is a very good one to put on your water altar because of its color. It can bring you healing, protection, and good luck. If you don't want to use crystals or you can't get them at the moment, then you should consider getting some dirt or sand from a swamp, riverside, or beach.

If you like, you can work with botanicals and flowers found in swampy or watery conditions. For instance, sea holly is a prickly yet pretty plant that you can find by the seaside. It brings you safety and love. The coconut isn't a nut, and it's not a fruit either. Known as a drupe, the coconut contains water that you can use on your altar to represent the water element or for your incense. The gardenia is a delicate white flower used in rituals of devotion, love, and spiritual connection. Eucalyptus is a watery herb that gives you focus, health, and psychic abilities as well.

Air

To represent air, you can use incense. Incense is one of the most common ways to represent this element. If you like, you could opt for one that's a blended craft correlating to one of the water zodiac signs — Cancer, Pisces, or Scorpio. Alternatively, you could decide to work with any of the previously mentioned botanicals in whatever combo you like by burning them on charcoal. The smoke from the incense is essentially air.

Fire

For fire, you can simply have a lit candle on your altar. You could opt for a white candle or a blue one. These candles could be blessed and dressed in oils and herbs that belong to the element of water. Another option is using a figural candle shaped in the form of a water deity like Tiamit, Neptune, or the Morrigan. Keep in mind that these deities all have their likes and dislikes, so make sure that all the other items on your altar respect that so that your magic can be very effective.

Water

For your water altar, it is obvious that water is one of the most important elements to have. Know that the kind of water you use has special properties and blessings. If you want to work the magic that involves new beginnings, then spring water works best. Want to create powerful change in your life or for someone else? Then use *stormwater*. If you constantly deal with obstacles and situations that throw you for a loop, then use river water to address them. If you're working very deep and meaningful magic, go for ocean water. Don't stress out about not having access to these. You can work with whatever water you have available, understanding that what matters the most is your clear intention.

If you can incorporate a fountain into your altar, you should absolutely do so to take advantage of the magic of moving water. You may put the water in a glass, bowl, bottle, chalice, or a calabash (if you've got one of those!) Water in motion has special attributes that give your spells extra power and efficacy.

Spirit

For spirit, you could simply incorporate a Water Goddess or God, or you can put an item that's special and represents your association with water on your altar. Sand, shells, or water you've collected can be used to represent spirit if you like. You could even opt for good old-fashioned tap water. Tap water is the water you have the most interactions with every day, and it very likely comes from a body of water close to you. The fact that it is close means it's powerful, so don't be too quick to dismiss tap water.

If you prefer, you could use items from water animals that you find very meaningful. You could use a feather, bones you harvested respectfully and responsibly, some water art, or a statue. Allow your intuition to guide you on what would make the best representation of spirit for your altar.

Putting It All Together

When you have everything you need, it's time to set up your shrine or altar. To be clear, your altar is a space that is sacred to you and should be treated as such. If you don't have a space you can use permanently, that's alright. You can simply clear the energy of space when you're ready to work magic. To do that, sage it or spray it with seawater or saltwater from a spray bottle as you intend that the energy around the area be sanctified. The objective of setting your altar up is to use it for the time being to manifest the intention you have. For instance, you might want to draw on the ability of water to help one deal with emotions, so creating an altar for this purpose can be quite rewarding.

A more permanent setup for your practice would be a *shrine,* where you regularly go to do your magic, rituals, and rites and leave offerings for the deities you resonate with the most. It doesn't matter the kind of space you want to set up. What's important is that it's somewhere you can access easily. However, it must be somewhere where your enemies, children, pets, and other distractions will have zero interaction.

Some people like to set up their water shrine or altar by setting down a blue cloth on which they then place the elemental items. Know that traditionally, the elements have their own cardinal directions. Earth belongs to the North, fire to the South, air to the East, and water to the West. So, you need to place the items in the right positions. You can set the item that represents ether or spirit in the center of the others. Whatever you do, you should find joy in creating your shrine or altar; this is a powerful practice in itself, allowing you to infuse your rituals with your unique intentions. As any true magician will tell you, the power of magic truly lies *with intentions*. There's no better way to make them clear and strong than to be deliberate in creating a sacred space for your magic.

Significance of Water Altars

Think of your water altar as a place where you can give honor to the power of water and all the good it does for you each day. It's where you can send messages to your gods and goddesses. It allows you to share how you feel, pray to them, and manifest whatever you want. With your water altar, you can connect to spiritual realms, listen to what your guides have to say, and deepen your relationships with the spirits of water. Your altar is a reflection of how you deal with every aspect of your life. When you meditate there, you will receive all the insight and inspiration you need to make your world the way you want it to be.

When creating your altar, it's important to trust your intuition. Think about what the element of water seems to require of you in particular. Take note of your emotions and thoughts as you set up your altar as well – an extremely important step because water has a way of recording your intentions, memories, and energy. It will store everything you're feeling and thinking, and for this reason, you want to make sure your head is clear and focused only on what you desire and nothing negative. If you're not in the right headspace to create your altar, then don't do it. Wait until you feel moved, and be intentional throughout the process. Intend clarity and power, and you will find that your altar will bring you those qualities. You will be able to work your spells with a clear mind, and they will have the power to bring about whatever change you desire.

Think about where you want your water altar to be. Do you want it outdoors in nature? Would you rather have it in your home? Where would work best for you? Your altar could be in your kitchen, temple, garden, bedroom, or living room. Also, think about the location of the room you choose. While not absolutely required, it does help if you pick a room in the west wing of your home. If you don't want to use blue cloth, you could choose white, purple, gold, green, or any other color that you feel would be the best for your altar.

Cleansing the Space

You must keep the energy around your altar clean and clear. With time, other energies can gather there, or the place might feel a bit stagnant. The reason you need to pay attention to this is that it can impact your rituals negatively. If you're working in a shrine or with an altar that you alone have access to, then you don't have to worry too much about this (although you should still remain alert to how the place feels). However, if you don't live alone or your space is one where others come around, you should cleanse the altar before performing your rituals. You can do this by smudging the place with any incense like copal, cedar, sage, or any other incense that feels right to you.

Consecrating Water

You should use consecrated water on your altar. It helps when you're intentional about your search for the right kind of water that calls to you, but it's completely fine to use tap water, as I mentioned before. You can collect water from the rain or a puddle around your home. It's really not about working with the cleanest and purest water, but about working with the element itself. Regardless of where your water comes from, the important thing to do is to consecrate it; you must collect it intentionally and then imbue it with your energy and desires. You could simply hold your hands over the water and pray over it or speak into the water. If you're worried about the source not being "pure" enough, remember that ultimately, all water comes from a powerful, pure, and pristine source. So, focus on that.

Once you've collected the water, you can sit with it in silence and feel its power. Ask your water deity or elemental to infuse this water with good energy, power, healing, blessings, and magic. You can even make offerings to the water if you would like, whether that's in the form of a song or dance, a crystal, an act of service, or anything else. The point of this offering is to express your gratitude for the magic and power that the water freely provides you. As you pour the water into your calabash, chalice, or whatever container you'll use on your altar, pay attention to the sound that it makes. Bask in it, and bless the water. Ask that it helps you, heals you, and cleanses you in every aspect of life. Speak with the water as you would a powerful friend who wants nothing but the best for you and to whom you're very grateful for all they do for you. Continue to converse with the water until you're overcome with a deep sense of appreciation, love, magic, and contentment.

Never underestimate the power of expressing gratitude to the water you use in your magic. You see, gratitude encourages life force — the stuff that creates all things — to flow through you and enrich your life. As you feel gratitude, you will be even more connected with the very source of life. You can direct that energy to do whatever it is you desire. You know you're truly feeling gratitude when even your body seems to sing with energy, pouring from your heart and flowing outwards.

It's good practice to renew and replace this water at least once a week to maintain its power and energy. If you don't keep this up, you might notice that the rest of your life begins to feel stagnant. Maintain this relationship with your altar water, and you'll notice how it affects every other aspect of your life. You will receive direct access to the wisdom of Infinite Intelligence, and it will guide you in all your ways and through all your days. It will feel like you have divine energy as a friend, constantly showing you where to go and what to do to get what you seek.

If you like, you can keep the water from the last week in a sacred bowl to mix it with fresh water. The reason this is a good practice is that you'll be incorporating all the energy and intentions that you've imbued that water with into the new water. The more you mix the old with the new each week, the more powerful the water becomes. When you feel like it's time to start afresh with completely new water, you can sprinkle this water in and around your home to bless and consecrate it, or you can feed it to your plants. They'll absolutely love it.

One final thing to note is that there is no right or wrong way to set up your altar or work with water. The important thing is that you work with what resonates with your soul. Take note of the results you get when you do things a certain way, and write them down in a grimoire so that you can always remember what works and what doesn't.

Chapter Five: Water Magic Crystals, Plants, and Herbs

Suppose you want to add more power and beauty to your altar and practice. In that case, you should definitely incorporate crystals, plants, and herbs. If you like, you can wear them as jewelry, add them to your gris-gris bags, put them beneath your pillow, use them to create a magical grid, or work with them however you like. You will feel their influence and power each day, and you won't want to live without them when you begin working with them.

Crystals

Some gemstones and crystals like amber are connected to water because they started in liquid form. Other stones are considered water stones because of their color, whether the ocean's blue, green, black, or white, depending on the time of day. Some crystals are connected to the element of water because they were created in the water. Having said that, you should know that not all crystals will work well when placed in water, and some of them can even become toxic. Ensure you become fully aware of what is safe to put in water and what isn't if you plan to have a bath with or take a drink of crystal water. Now, let's take a look at the crystals that are connected to water.

Amber is not really a stone but a plant resin that is hardened. You can get amber from insects and plants that have been trapped in it if you like. When combined with jet, amber is seen as the witch's stone. Amber is the stone to work with when you desire wisdom, love, protection, healing, beauty, longevity, and purification. It's also lovely for creating and restoring balance to your sacral chakra. This stone works as a healing and protective charm for children, particularly when they're teething, but that doesn't mean you should let your baby eat it. Oshun and Freya both hold amber sacred.

Alexandrite is another form of beryl, and the stone to work with when you want to manifest your desires, improve your intuition and psychic abilities, increase creativity, and bring joy into your life. Of all the gems, it's one of the hardest ever. It's a pretty rare stone, and sometimes it can be even pricier than diamonds. When you carry this stone around with you, you tap directly into the power of the Divine, and you will notice that you have good luck in everything you do.

Azurite is a blue crystal that looks absolutely beautiful and magical. This deep blue stone is definitely connected to water. It's the stone you should use when you want peace, calm, emotional healing, insight, clarity, and intuition. It's also a great stone for meditation and astral projection. Even though it's associated with water, please keep this stone out of the water, or else it will fall apart. You can use this to work with your throat, heart, and crown chakras.

Amethyst is a beautiful stone for gaining insight into all situations and connecting you with spiritual realms. The great Leonardo da Vinci was convinced that this stone could boost your intelligence. Work with it when you want happiness, self-love, spiritual connections, mental clarity, romance, and self-awareness.

Blue Calcite is a lovely stone. Like all calcite forms, it can help you with physical, emotional, and spiritual growth –the stone to use when you want psychic knowledge, vision, success, courage, hope, and creativity. It also helps you become a better communicator and makes you more receptive to important messages. If you want to balance your crown and throat chakras, you can place blue calcite on them. You can put a piece of this beneath your bed or pillow if you want to have prophetic dreams and remember them clearly. To keep your home safe from thieves, you can keep one at the front door or anywhere else within your home.

Beryl is a family of stones. Stones such as alexandrite, morganite, aquamarine, bixbite, emerald, and others form part of this family. Beryls have been valued for several millennia. They bring harmony in relationships, hope, happiness, and healing. It also keeps you and your space safe from evil spirits and demons. Morganite is great for healing your heart and heart chakra. Bixbite can help you heal your body's aura and open up your chakras so that they flow and are balanced. Blue aquamarine will give you courage and is great if you're a sensitive person. It helps you become more tolerant and less judgmental. If you feel like you've got too much on your plate, it offers strength and support.

Blue Chalcedony is a great stone to improve your meditation practice. It will bring you harmony in spirit, body, and mind. When you want to remember your past lives, be better at communicating, or activate your throat chakra, blue chalcedony will help you. Some people give this stone to their children to help them overcome nervousness, fear, and anxiety. This stone can be found in Madagascar, Brazil, Turkey, and India.

Blue Topaz is good for intelligence, good fortune, healing, beauty, long life, and self-love. It's also known as the "writer's stone," as it gets rid of writer's block and is shown to improve creativity. You can also use this to improve the flow of energy in your third eye and throat chakras.

Coral is from the ocean itself and has many varieties. Each one has its unique properties. Blue coral can help you with psychic abilities, communication, diplomacy, commerce, and healing. You can use this stone to energize your throat, navel, and third eye chakras. Black coral is great for getting rid of negative entities and toxins from your body. It is a protective stone that can give you confidence and also help you solve problems. Red coral is good for improving friendships and fostering ties between individuals in groups and communities. It helps with building optimism, enthusiasm, and passion. It can also help with kidney and bladder issues.

Chrysocolla has various forms. The most common one is a bright greenish-blue hue, but it could also be black or brown. This stone helps you with communication in every way. It's the stone to get when you want to be more courageous about speaking your truth no matter what. You can use this to heal your throat chakra or bring it back into balance. It's great for your heart chakra too. This stone can help you lovingly connect with others. You can find it in abundance in Arizona, New Mexico, Utah, and Pennsylvania. Usually, it's mixed with malachite, quartz, and other crystals.

Green Calcite is a stone that can help correct mental imbalance, nervousness, and anxiety. If you have a challenging time letting go of things and people who no longer serve you, this stone will assist you. You can also use this stone to help you work through trust issues and heal yourself in various ways. You must ensure that you cleanse this stone spiritually as often as you can. The same can be said of other stones.

Emerald is one of the beryl stones. It's quite lovely and is associated with Vishnu, Isis, and Ceres. Also, Thoth has his emerald tablets which have deep magical mysteries and wisdom for us all. The emerald is the stone that brings you psychic visions, healing from emotional trauma, and good luck. It's known as the "stone of truth." As this stone is associated with the heart chakra, it improves your partnerships and relationships. If you notice a sudden change in the stone's color, it means your significant other has been dishonest or unfaithful. This gem is about finding balance within yourself and in the way you relate with others.

Jet is a stone that can turn any tough situation around. It works just like an energy filter, with the ability to purify your space and protect you. You can use a jet to clean and cleanse other stones and your ritual space as well. If you feel stuck financially, you can carry a jet stone in your wallet to energetically eliminate all the blocks holding you back from prosperity.

Jade is a stone with diverse colors, but the one connected to water is the green one. It represents love in every form, from romantic love to self-love and divine love. It is connected to Kwan Yin, who is known to be one of the most compassionate and loving goddesses. The jade is a lucky stone that can bring insight and clarity in all that you do.

The moon and water rule the moonstone. Use this stone when you want joy, happiness, love, insight, and a mind that welcomes serendipity. You can put this under your pillow or wear it to experience calm if you're dealing with troublesome thoughts and emotions.

Lapis Lazuli is a beautiful stone that's often used for general magic and water magic. You can use this for connection, psychic power, healing, and love.

Opal has various forms, but the hyalite opal is connected to water. The stone brings you joy, hope, and luck. It is the stone that boosts psychic connections and will bring you incredible insight.

Obsidian is formed from molten lava that cooled quickly and became a crystal. The most common obsidian is black, but it could also be green, blue, or brown. It could also have a gold or silver sheen to it. Just like water, the obsidian is a stone that reveals the unknown and the hidden. It can remove negative energy, get rid of depression, eliminate blockages, and help you process difficult emotions. This stone is connected to the zodiac sign Scorpio.

Peridot has a distinct green color. Its name comes from the Greek word *peridona*, which means "abundance." This stone will keep you safe from the evil eye. It has been highly valued not just for its beauty but its ability to bring you love, friendship, clarity, protection, and success for thousands of years.

Riverstone is connected to limestone. It can be found worldwide and will bring you happiness, success, luck, and emotional healing. This stone will bring change in your life quickly and effectively. Wear this stone when you need some mental or physical rejuvenation.

River Agate comes in various forms, and they are usually named after the water sources they are found in. For instance, you have Lake Superior Agate, Savannah River Fairyland Agate, China Lake Plume Agate, Cave Creek Agate, and others. This stone will bring you success, love, luck, good relationships, and harmony.

Rose Quartz is a crystal that can allow you to connect with love on both a divine and personal level. It's a great stone for healing and friendship as well. Also known as the heart stone, this has always been regarded as a love talisman. It's connected with water and can help you both access and process your true emotions. The rose quartz is often presented as an offering to Yemoja, Isis, Venus, Hathor, Freya, and other gods and goddesses. This stone is deeply connected to the divine feminine.

Sodalite is a blue stone connected with water, and it's a good one to use when you want to speak truth to power. This stone will help you establish a deep connection between your thoughts and emotions. Sometimes, people mistake it for lapis lazuli, but the latter has golden highlights and flecks. This stone can help you transform your life and move you where you need to be to experience the best version of yourself.

Sardonyx is in parts of Asia, India, Brazil, and Russia. You can use this stone to make your space full of optimism, joy, and courage.

Sugilite was first found in Japan in 1944, but it's now a very popular stone. Sugilite will connect your head with your heart, and it heals your crown and heart chakras. Use this when you need to balance out your actions and words with loving intention.

Turquoise is a very intense blue, and it's directly connected with water. This stone results from water pushing through aluminum and copper deposits and can offer you luck, joy, healing, and longevity. It is valued among Egyptians, Native Americans, and other cultures. The word turquoise is etymologically French and translates to "Turkish." Quite the cosmopolitan stone, isn't it?

Plants, Botanicals, and Herbs

Water plants and herbs are connected to water in several ways. You have herbs connected to the water signs of Scorpio, Cancer, and Pisces, as well as the moon. You also have plants and herbs that represent water because they thrive and grow in watery environments or in the water itself. Finally, some botanicals are considered water correspondents because they have very juicy sap or fruit. We will get into some of these, but know that this list is far from exhaustive. You can add any other plants or herbs that you intuitively sense are connected to water.

You must be aware that you might get a negative reaction if you ingest some of these plants and herbs or use them topically or as essential oils. You should never ingest or use them without checking in with a licensed medical practitioner first. Please be very careful when working with botanicals you're not familiar with. Let's look at a few now.

Apples are traditionally offered to Sango, Santa Muerte, Hecate, Hel, and Lilith. You can work with the fruit itself, the bark of the tree, or the flower. It is connected to Jupiter and Venus, so you can use it when working magic associated with these planets. Apples represent knowledge. Also, when you slice them open horizontally, you will find a five-pointed star much like the pentacle, a revered symbol in witchcraft. Use apples for passion, romance, psychic connection, healing, and divination.

Aloe Vera is an amazing plant for healing. You can have it as a supplement or a drink, or you can use it topically. That said, you should know that it can be toxic at certain levels, so ensure you do sufficient research on what's safe for you and use it with caution. Ninety-six percent of this plant is water, so it's naturally connected to the element. This plant has been a very popular medicinal herb for at least 2,000 years. Having a live one in your home will keep you safe from mishaps and accidents. In some parts of Africa, it's hung close to windows and doors to ward off the evil eye. Sacred to Aphrodite and Venus, you can offer it to them in your shrine or on your altar. Use this to work beauty and love spells.

Bay Leaves are powerful. It's used in Hoodoo and kitchen witchery. If you want prosperity and riches, you can write your intention on it and then burn it. You can write your lover's name and carry that leaf around in your pocket to keep your love secure and stimulate growth. You can also write the names of those who hate you and burn those leaves to rid yourself of their influence and presence in your life. The bay is a popular houseplant. Growing the tree in your home will keep you safe from accidents and thieves. The Orisas Babalu Aye and Obatala hold this plant sacred.

Catnip is holy to Aphrodite, Freya, and Bast. It's a fun recreational drug for cats, but it works well for love rituals for us. It works as an attractant for attracting what you desire and is a fantastic addition to spells meant to bring love to your life and passion in your bedroom. You can add it to your baths, oils, and washes to amplify its power.

Coconut is very common and useful. It's great for cleansing, purification, prosperity, and blessings. The La Regla Lucumi practitioners often use it in their ritual baths and washes. This is sacred to Elegua and Yemoja.

German Chamomile is associated with the Fae and their magic. Use it to bring you gentle love, protection, luck, peaceful sleep, calm, and relaxation.

Cypress is a plant that loves to grow in water. You can find it in swamps and other watery places. It brings you success, wealth, protection, healing, and blessings. Offer cypress to Athena, Hera, Hecate, Aphrodite, Astarte, Yemoja, Oya, and Nana Buruku.

Cucumber is a common veggie that we've cultivated for at least 3,000 years. It's also made up of about 96 percent water, much like aloe vera, so it's definitely one of the water plants. You can use this for healing, love, and lust spells. Putting cucumber slices on your eyes not only helps with those nasty eye bags from lack of sleep but can also promote better psychic visions as well.

Eucalyptus is a healing herb. It also helps with balance, clarity, focus, concentration, psychic ability, and divination. You can use it with magical work that involves calming panic attacks and anxiety. This is the plant of the Orisas Babalu Aye and Obatala.

Heather is also known as Scotch heather or ling. You can find it in North America, Greenland, Asia, and Europe. It is used for making baskets, brushes, and brooms, and in the Scottish Highland, it was used as a building material. Its botanical name is Calluna vulgaris. Calluna is from Kalluno, a Greek word that means "to cleanse." You can use small heather bundles by tying them together to make scourges or brooms for ritual washes and cleansing baths.

Gardenias are white flowers that represent purity, devotion, spiritual connection, and love. These flowers are sacred to Hecate, Aphrodite, Obatala, Kwan Yin, and Isis. As they are connected to love magic, you'll find them in wedding flower arrangements often. Add gardenia oil to your ritual oils, floor washes, and baths, or simply put the flowers themselves on your altar or in your shrine. It's super easy to grow it at home, both indoors and out.

Hyacinth is a fragrant flower that blooms in purple, blue, yellow, white, and pink. You can use them for peace of mind, calm, happiness, joy, removing negativity, and freeing yourself from oppression; this is Yemoja's flower.

Jasmine has over 200 species. Its name is etymologically Persian, and it means "gifts from God." The plant is great for happiness, joy, love, healing, psychic connection, divination, and abundance. Use it to heal your heart chakra and balance its energy flow. It's sacred to Orunla, Venus, Ishtar, Hecate, Diana, Bast, Aphrodite, and Aine. This plant belongs to the moon and is poetically referred to as "moonlight on the grove."

Lemon Balm is an herb that is sacred to Yemoja and Artemis. Use this when working rituals involving joy, passion, love, wisdom, calm, and strength.

Lemon is sacred to Yemoja, Luna, and Juno. According to folk magic, you should put a slice of lemon beneath each person's chair at dinner so that your guests will remain at peace with each other. Magically, you can work with its fruit, leaves, or juice. You can use this to bless yourself and others in love and romance, foster peace, cause joy, purify, and protect.

Lilac is a favorite of the Orisas Yemoja and Osun and Maman Brigitte, the cemetery's Iwa. It can chase ghosts away from your home and properties and can bring positive energy and protection. Use this flower to gain knowledge about your past lives and for divination.

Licorice is used in lots of confectioneries and medicines. If you're pregnant, a nursing mom, or dealing with heart issues, you need to consult your doctor before you use it. This is good for spells that involve controlling, compelling, and commanding. However, you might find working with this a bit problematic, so you need to be careful. You can use it for magic that involves love, passion, and dealing with the dead. If you're going to grow it at home, you need to make sure you soak the seeds properly so that they can sprout faster and produce a greater yield.

Lobelia is a favorite of the Fae. You can use them for weather magic, cleansing, protection, love, and romance. If there's a storm coming, throw this in the direction of the storm, and it will change course.

Lilies have many species, like calla lilies, water lilies, daylilies, and others. Each sort has its peculiar magic. You can use daylilies when you need to forget your worries and help you with childbirth and parenting. They are connected to Osun, Obatala, Venus, Juno, Hera, and the Virgin Mary. You can incorporate them into rituals for love, fertility, passion, progress, hope, development, faith, remembrance, and renewal. They're effective for communicating with the dead as well.

Lotus flowers can be used for divination, healing, meditation, and protection. You can offer this to Osun, Yemoja, and Isis.

Nettle is also known as devil's plaything, burn weed, or burn hazel. This plant stings. You can use it for exorcisms, protection, removing jinxes, and breaking hexes.

Passionflower is used to bring sensual pleasure, love, and passion. Many plants have this same name, but they all work to remove illness and negativity. They also align your energy to higher levels and give you access to psycho knowledge. This plant is a sacred offering Sango, an Orisa.

Orris Root is used for romance, love, protection, and healing the heart. Use this to balance and clean out your heart chakra and as an offering to Orunla and Elegua.

Pomegranates are connected to the underworld and Persephone. Some say that the forbidden fruit in the Garden of Eden wasn't an apple but a pomegranate. This fruit is used in spells regarding prosperity, fertility, money, abundance, divination, protection, wisdom, and knowledge. You can also use the juice to replace blood in certain rituals and potions. It is sacred to Sekhmet, Persephone, and Astarte.

Periwinkle is also known as the Sorcerer's violet. This flower can bring you success, money, harmony, calm, peace, passion, love, and psychic awareness. Folk magic has it that if you have lost your child, you should plant this on their grave so that you can heal and remember the good times with them.

Peaches are very valuable in Chinese culture, where it's believed that they offer vitality. The fruit, wood, and blossoms are useful when it comes to working magic. You can use its wood to make dowsing rods and wands. Consuming the fruit can bring love to you, and is sacred to Osun, Venus, Hathor, Freya, and Aphrodite. Use these in magic for fertility, sensual desires, passion, romance, and longevity.

Rose of Jericho is a plant that can spring back to life when you put it in water, and this is why it's also called the resurrection plant. Rose of Jericho is good for renewing anything stagnant or dead: love, health, business, or finances.

Roses represent love in most cultures. You can offer them to Santa Muerte, Isis, Demeter, Hecate, Hathor, Freya, Adonis, Pomba Gira, Yemoja, and Osun. You can also use it to work rituals that involve luck, healing, psychic connection, divination, purification, protection, luck, and more. According to Islamic and Jewish lore, the rose can reveal the truth of a situation. Since it takes about 2,000 roses to make 1 gram of rose oil, you might find it better to use rose water instead for your washes and baths. You can also get food-grade rose water to incorporate into your meals. If you cook with this, you'll foster a deep sense of love in all who partake of that meal.

Spearmint is also known as yerba buena in Spanish, which means "good herb." This is used for love, fortitude, clarity, protection, healing, psychic knowledge, and spiritual cleansing. It's part of the mint family and is called spearmint because its leaves resemble little spears. You can use this in rituals to banish bad energy and negativity and offer it to Yemoja, Sango, Elegua, Pluto, and Aphrodite.

Sage has at least 1,000 species, with the common sage used in meals. You can use white sage for rituals. If you're a pregnant woman or nursing mother, you should know that sage can cut down your milk supply. It's great for working with your third eye, sacral, and crown chakras. You can also use it to banish negativity and nightmares, eliminate ego traps, receive clarity, attract money, and ground yourself. It's connected to Jupiter, Zeus, Hecate, Brigid, Elegua, and Obatala.

Sweet Peas come in violet, red, pink, white, or purple. They are used in spells for affection, love, friendship, and breaking down undesired defenses. They can be offered to Osun.

Thyme is mainly used for cooking but can also be used in rituals for affection, love, loyalty, healing, courage, romance, psychic power, divination, protection, grief, and legal problems. Ancient Egyptians would use it in funeral rituals. In contrast, ancient Roman military leaders and statesmen would eat it to keep themselves from being poisoned. Thyme is also connected to the Fae.

Tansy is part of the daisy family and can be used to promote longevity and immortality. You should be careful with this as it contains thujone, a toxic chemical. This herb can keep you safe from diseases and sickness, and it can be used as a smudge to keep your home clean and protected. The Virgin Mary holds this one sacred.

Tonka beans are great for manifesting your deepest wishes and desires. Use them for love, partnership, and romance.

Violet comes in purple, yellow, or white. You can use them to grant you peace, serenity, simplicity, lust, love, and luck. Violets are connected to children and the Fae, and you can also use them for good dreams and a peaceful night's rest.

Vanilla is magically associated with communication, clarity, beauty, healing, joy, love, empowerment, psychic knowledge, and energy. It is sacred to Osun, Elegua, Hecate, and Lilith.

Valerian is also known as vandal root and is used for harmony, healing, calm, sleep, strength, and turning bad into good. You can offer it to Venus, Hertha, and Aphrodite.

Willow is the material used to make witch's brooms or besoms. You can use them to make wonderful dowsing rods as well. Connected to the moon, it is sacred to Maman Brigitte, Selena, Luna, Persephone, Hecate, Diana, Cerridwen, Brighid, and Artemis. Use this for empathy, divination, psychic dreams, grief, astral travel, enchantment, and healing. You can also use it to create a loving, calm, and gentle atmosphere.

White Sandalwood is used for psychic connection, purification, protection, success, healing, and joy. It is ruled by the moon and can be used in spells connected to it. You can offer this to Lilith, Venus, and Freya, as well as the Orisas Yemoja, Sango, and Oya. Burn it as incense or resin to purify your space or magical tools. Its incense can also help you focus and meditate. Keep in mind that this herb, particularly the Indian sandalwood, is going extinct due to overharvesting. So be mindful about your purchase and your use of it.

Ylang-Ylang is also known as the "flower of flowers." It can be used to bring true love, intense passion, opportunity, foresight, success, and joy. Use it to elevate your magical practice. You can offer it to Osun and Elegua.

Chapter Six: Lir — Water in Celtic Magic

The Children of Lir are from an old Irish legend from the epoch after Christianization that combines druidic spells, magical elements, and Christianity's message of providing the only way out of suffering. In Irish, the story is named Oidheadh Chloinne Lir, but it's now known as the Children of Lir. It's also called The Tragic Story of the Children of Lir, among other titles.

This is a very sad story about a family's love, jealousy, magic, and a 900-year-old curse. Once upon a time in Ireland, people called the Tuatha De Danaan lived before Gael's time. These people were a mystical race who had powerful magic and were ruled by King Bodh Dearg. Their king was wise and fair in all his dealings, but Lir, one of his nobles, utterly disliked him.

The king was aware that Lir harbored an intense hatred towards him. However, he had enough wisdom to know that it was more important to maintain the peace in his kingdom and keep everyone united. So, to assuage Lir, the king gave him one of his daughters to marry.

The king's plan worked. Lir was happy that he got to choose one of two of the king's most beautiful daughters. He chose Aoibh. While the marriage started as a matter of convenience, Lir and Aoibh came to love each other deeply. With time, they had a beautiful daughter they named Fionnuala, and three good-looking sons named Fiachra, Conn, and Aedh. This was a happy family full of love, but their joy was not to last.

Tragedy Strikes

Aoibh took ill and eventually died, leaving her children brokenhearted; it utterly ruined Lir's heart as well. King Bodh Dearg was amazed at just how much his daughter's family loved one another. For this reason, he decided to give Lir his second daughter to marry. Her name was Aoife. Lir had assumed that Aoife would be like her sister, gentle and kind in all her ways. So, he accepted her. He had hoped with all his heart that he and his children would come to love Aoife as deeply as they had Aoibh.

Aoife's Jealousy

Aoife was certainly beautiful, no doubt about it. However, she was nowhere near as kind as Aoibh was. She noticed that her husband was so utterly devoted to his kids, and she could see how fiercely the kids loved him as well. She didn't like this at all. In fact, she gradually began to burn with jealous rage.

You see, Aoife wasn't in the habit of sharing. She wanted Lir to love her and her alone, so she deeply despised her nephews and niece. Her hatred took firm roots in her heart and poisoned her thoughts so much that she came to a horrible conclusion when she and the kids were on their way back from Bodh Dearg's home one day. She conceived the thought that the children must die.

A Spell Is Cast

Aoife had ordered her servant to kill her stepchildren, but the servant wouldn't do it. So, Aoife took it on herself to commit the deed. However, she quickly realized that her courage for such a cruel act was not nearly as strong as her hatred. So, she decided she'd rather do it as cleanly as possible. She chose to kill them with magic instead.

So, Aoife summoned all the power she could muster to cast a spell on those helpless, defenseless children. The result? She turned them into swans. Not only that, but she had also bound them to dwell on the Lough Derravaragh (Loch Daibhreach) waters for 300 years and to spend another 300 years on the Struth na Maoile (or the Straits of Moyle). They were to remain in flight between the coasts of Alba and Eire.

However, even after the allotted 600 years had gone by, they weren't free from this curse. They had another 300 years to spend on Inis Gluaire (or Inish Glora) and Iorus Domnann, the wild western seas. She had set up the spell so that no one could lift it, and nothing would break it until the children heard a bell ring that announced a new religion.

Bodh Dearg's Outrage

When Bodh darg learned of what had become of his grandchildren, he absolutely lost it. He was so livid that it was a miracle he didn't just end Aoife on the spot when she had gone to see him. However, he decided that a swift death would be too kind for her. Collecting himself, he decided to deal with her in the same way she had destroyed his grandkids' life. He would give her the same medicine: Magic. He cast her as far away from him and all of humanity by transforming her into an air demon.

For 300 years, the four children, now swans, had lived on the Loch Daibhreach's calm waters. They would have the sweet grasses from the field for food and eat the lake's fish. Their father continued to love them the whole time and would stay with them till it was time for him to rejoin Aoibh and leave the world. Once again, the children were heartbroken.

Eventually, it was time for the swans to head northeast to Maoile, the stormy stream where the cold northern gales would sweep through. There they remained for 300 years more, and they lived on Scotland's and Ireland's wrecked and wretched shores. This time, they had no father to give them comfort. All they had was each other.

A Bell Rings

Then came the time for the children of Lir to head West. They spent another miserable 300 years feeding on fish on the coasts of the stormy, terrible sea, living day to day overwhelmed by gut-wrenching sorrow. However, one day, something would change.

The four swan children were busy eating when there was a noise. It was a clanging sound, loud but pleasant. They'd never heard any sound like it their whole lives, but they knew right away what it was. If you'd asked them how they knew, they wouldn't be able to say. It just struck them that this was definitely a bell ringing. They realized that they'd just heard the sound of freedom. So, they swam in the direction of the noise and soon saw someone heading toward them along the shore.

The person on the shore looked nothing like the people they'd known all their lives. This person was definitely from anywhere but Tuatha De Danaan. He had a head shaved on the top, and he wore a habit that looked rough and homespun, fastened around his waist with a rope. They said hello to this stranger, shocking him. When he recovered, he immediately wanted to know who they were. They then told him about their misfortunes, forced on them by their evil aunt. He felt moved with love and pity for their plight and let them know his name: Caomhog.

A New Religion in Eire

At this point, the De Dannan no longer lived on the land. They had moved into the sidhe underworld. The land was now held by the Gael's children, which meant the old gods were no longer in charge, as Saint Patrick had arrived in Eire to bring the people news of Christ the savior and one true God.

Caomhog, a monk, told the children to follow him to his domicile so that he could care for them until the day the curse was officially broken. They agreed to come along. Then the monk gave them an explanation of the new religion that had replaced the old.

Then, one day, came a warrior. He yelled about being Lairgnen, king of Connacht. He asked that the swan people be given to Deoch, his new wife, as a wedding gift. Caomhog refused and scolded the king, telling him that he wouldn't have the swans in no uncertain terms. Then Caomhog rang his bell once again, and right away, the swans' feathers fell off their bodies, and they became human once more.

After this happened, the children of Lir's bodies began to age rapidly. The centuries they'd been alive for were finally catching up with them. Lairgnen was terrified when he saw this, so he fled. However, the aging children asked Caomhog to baptize them, as they knew they would soon be no more. Fionnuala gave the monk explicit instructions on how to bury them. She was put in the middle. Conn and Fiachra were on either side of their sister, and Aedh was in her front. This is how the four Tuatha De Danaan made their way into heaven.

When to Work with Lir

Lir is an Irish Sea God, also called Llyr or Ler. Other than the mythology of the children of Lir, it is believed that he shows up in Shakespeare's work as King Lear, and he just might be Leicester's god as well. He rules over the seas and oceans. Some say that he isn't exactly a sea god but is the sea personified. He is also known as Allod and seems to be connected to the Welsh Llyr. He is also the father of Manannan mac Lir, also known as Manann or Manannan, a king and warrior of the otherworld.

Sometimes, we find ourselves in situations that are extremely dire through no fault of our own. It can feel like life is completely against you. The ones you think should protect you and love you let you down, and sometimes, they're the ones with the knife in your back, twisting for all they're worth. In times like these, you can call on Lir, and he will answer you.

Just as Lir was there for his children to give them support, you can invoke him to feel his loving energy, give you hope, and help you keep your chin up while you go through uncomfortable times.

The Salmon of Wisdom

Another fascinating story from Irish mythology is that of the Salmon of Knowledge. It's a story about the greatest man in Ireland, Fionn Mac Cumhail. Irish mythology has it that Noah's son Bith, Cesair, his daughter, Fintan mac Bochra, her husband, and Ladhra were the first in Ireland. It was Ladhra who had led their ship to the island. They had also come with 50 virgins. With time, Ladhra took off on his own to find a path for himself, and Bith had passed away, so it was just Fintan, Cesair, and the 50 women all on their own. Fintan found this too much to bear. So, he left the women to their devices and went off on his own. Grieved because she had lost her men, Cesair soon died after a period of deep melancholy.

Shortly after she passed, there was a great Deluge. This flood had wiped the entire earth clean, leaving just Noah and his family in their ark, safe and sound. Thanks to God's mercy and deep sorrow for Fintan, he let him become a salmon so that he could survive the great flood.

The Salmon Becomes Knowledgeable

When all the water had receded considerably, Fintain, still a salmon, swam his way to the Boyne River. Soon, he found a deep pool that was nice and quiet, and he remained there to regain his strength. God had let nine haze trees grow around the pool. Each tree had exactly nine nuts on it, and the nuts had all the world's knowledge. Seasons passed, and soon it was autumn. These nuts of wisdom grew and matured, and they eventually fell one by one into the pool where Fintan swam. He ate each one as it hit the surface of the water, and in this way, he received all the world's wisdom. This is why he is called Bradan and Eolais, or An Bradan Feasa, which both mean "Salmon of Knowledge."

Many centuries passed. People went back to the land. They knew of the Salmon of Knowledge, but not one person had ever caught it, let alone received its wisdom. Then there was a druid poet named Finegas who settled in the Boyne valley. He had dreams of catching Fintan one day, so he could eat him and learn all there was to know about the world.

At this time in Ireland, there was the Fianna, a group of hero-warriors. One of them was Cumal, and he was the Fianna's leader. He fell in love with Murna, daughter of the druid Tadg mac Nuadat of the White Neck. However, her father wouldn't let them get married. Desperate, Cumal kidnaped Murna, and together they took off, heading as far away from Tadg as possible. Murna got pregnant and had a boy she named Demna. Tadg grew stark raving mad. He made sure Cumal was mercilessly killed in battle by the hand of Goll mac Morna. However, the baby was secreted away.

Demna became a fine young man and a brave one, too. He was so fair in countenance that he became known as Fionn rather than Demna. Later, he became Fionn Mac Cumhail. He had to remain vigilant as his grandfather Tadg was still out for blood, and Goll, who had become the leader of the Fianna. It was decided that the safe thing to do was to have Bodhmall the druidess and Fiacal mac Conchinn, her husband care for him. He then studied under the poet Finegas (Finn Eces).

The Salmon Is Captured

Fionn learned the druidic arts from Finegas, who never stopped believing that he would find and capture the Salmon of Knowledge one day. Each day, he cast his line into the Boyne River, thinking he would hook the fish. He didn't let his hope die, and eventually, fortune favored him. He cast his line as always, and this time around, he hooked the biggest salmon ever seen. He knew right away that there could only be one that huge. It was the one fish of his dreams.

Joyfully, Finegas dragged the salmon onto the riverbank. He called for Fionn and instructed him to build a fire and cook the fish right away. He sternly warned Fionn that he wasn't to eat the fish, and the boy promised he wouldn't do that.

Finegas was brimming with joy because not only would he be Ireland's wisest druid, but he would also be the wisest person on all the earth. He was so exhausted from all the excitement and his great accomplishment that he went to bed. Fionn set the salmon on a spit positioned over the fire and began cooking it. When it was almost done, he called Finegas to come and have his meal, but then some of the fish's burning fat splashed Fionn on the thumb, and it burned him badly. So, as you do when your fingers inadvertently touch something too hot, Fionn stuck his thumb in his mouth.

Finegas showed up ready to have a delicious meal of fish and infinite wisdom. However, he noticed that there was something very different about Fionn. His pupil didn't look right. He asked Fionn if he'd had the fish, and the boy said no. He then mentioned what had happened with the fat and his thumb. At that point, it hit Finegas that no matter how badly he wanted it, and no matter how close he'd come, it simply wasn't his destiny to have the Salmon's wisdom. That was always meant for Fionn Mac Cumhail. So, he let the boy have it, and that very night, Fionn became the greatest Irishman of all.

From then on, when Fionn would put his thumb in his mouth and recite the teinm laida, anything he wanted to know would be revealed to him. He used this "Thumb of Knowledge" to plot his revenge against Goll.

Working with the Salmon of Knowledge and Fionn Mac Cumhail

Just because Fionn got to eat the Salmon of Knowledge doesn't mean all that knowledge is forever inaccessible to you. You can incorporate the salmon into your water magic rituals when you need knowledge on a particular subject in school or about a situation you may be faced with in life. Alternatively, you could summon the spirit of Fionn Mac Cumhail respectfully and ask that he guide you in whatever you need help with.

Whether you choose to work with the Salmon of Knowledge or with Fionn Mac Cumhail, you must realize that once you've asked, you have been answered. The answer may not reveal itself to you right away, but keep your mind open, and it will come to you.

Answers can come through dreams or random conversations around you regarding what you want to know. You could get intuitive nudges to go somewhere, call someone, or do some research on a certain word or phrase.

The most common way I receive my answers is a word or name that suddenly pops in my head and won't go away no matter what unless and until I look it up. Very often, that word or name will lead me to the answer I seek.

Remember, you just need to keep your mind open, and the answer will come. Also, when you ask, forget about it completely as though the matter has already been resolved, and you will get the wisdom you need at the right place and the right time.

Chapter Seven: Water in Scottish Magick

Just like the Irish, the Scottish have very interesting mythology connected to water magic. It helps to know these stories to see what resonates with you when working water magic. You might feel an intuitive nudge to begin working with some of the characters or incorporate the story elements in your water magic. So, let's begin with one of the more popular stories.

Fingal's Cave

On Staffa, an uninhabited island in the Inner Hebrides, a huge sea cage is formed from hexagonal-shaped basalt columns. This structure is reminiscent of Northern Ireland's Giant's Causeway, and its acoustics are natural and magical. No one knows the origin of its name. Some believe that the cave was named after Fingal, the hero of a poem by James Macpherson, an 18th-century Scots poet-historian. Others say that Fingal or Finn Mac Cumhail was likely an Irish general who had loyal warriors. Supposedly, he was the father of Ossian, who was the Gaels' traditional bard. The Gaels had moved from Ireland to Scotland till the Norsemen began raiding the Scottish coast, and there are likely stories of Fingal in these raids. He was honored in Scotland with time, and it only made sense to name the cavern after him, especially in light of the Ossianic songs and hero verse.

There's another legend that Finn McCool, an Irish giant, was the one who built Giant's Causeway, which lies between Scotland and County Antrim. He supposedly did this because he wanted to cross the sea without his feet getting wet. Felix Mendelssohn is a Romantic composer who visited Fingal's Cave and composed an overture called The Hebrides (also called Fingal's Cave overture). The odd echoes within the cave inspired him. There's even a song by Pink Floyd called Fingal's Cave.

The Corryvreckan Whirlpool

This whirlpool got its name from the Gaelic phrase Coire Bhreacain, which means "cauldron of the plaid" or "cauldron of the speckled seas." It's also known as the Strait of Corryvreckan, which lies off mainland Scotland's west coast, between the islands of Scarba and Jura.

This whirlpool is the third-largest in the world. The inflow and flood tides to the west from the Firth of Lorn can drive the Corryvreckan waters to waves as high as or higher than 30 feet, and the roar that sounds, as a result, can be heard as far as 10 miles away. The sheer power of this whirlpool isn't just physical but magical as well, with the ability to amplify your water rituals as nothing else can.

Legend has it that Breacan, a Norse prince, had his boat moored close to the whirlpool because he had wanted to impress a local princess's father. The latter had asked him to remain anchored by the whirlpool for three consecutive days and nights. So, the prince had three ropes, one made of wool, one of hemp, and one of maiden's hair. Legend has it that the maidens' hair was great for making unbreakable rope, especially if the maiden was pure.

On the first night, Breacan was by the whirlpool, he used his hemp rope, but it snapped. On the second night, he used the one made of wool which also snapped, and on the final night, he used the rope of hair. It shouldn't have snapped, but it did. Then his boat went under. Only one crew member survived, and he dragged the prince's body onto the shore. One of the maidens was overcome with guilt. She confessed that contrary to what the prince assumed, she wasn't as pure as she seemed, which is why the rope broke.

The Nine Maidens of Dundee

There was a farmer who dwelled with nine lovely daughters on Pitempton, a farm. After a busy day of farming, he asked his eldest daughter to go to a well nearby and fetch some water. When she didn't return after a while, he sent his second eldest after her. When the second also didn't return, he sent his third eldest. On and on, he sent his girls from eldest to youngest until all his daughters were gone.

The farmer went to the well to see what the problem was. What he found was tragic. All his daughters had been gruesomely slain, their bodies discarded across the ground. Wrapped around their badly battered bodies and basking in blood was a huge dragon that resembled a serpent. Afraid that he would become the dragon's tenth meal, he took off for dear life, calling out to his neighbors for help. They returned with weapons to kill the dragon.

When the dragon realized it couldn't possibly beat the mob, it tried to escape, but there was a young man called Martin who caught up with it. With only a wooden club, he beat the dragon to death as the crowd egged him on, yelling, "Strike, Martin!" So it was that the place of the dragon's defeat was named Strike-Martin, and then later renamed Strathmartine.

The Loch Ness Monster

In 1934, a doctor from London took a picture of what looked like a dinosaur coming out of the water, making many believe that the creature likely was the last survivor of all the plesiosaurs long since extinct. The water plesiosaurs were believed to have died over 65 million years ago, along with other dinosaurs. Since Loch Ness was solid ice all through the recent ice ages, the monster would have had to journey from the sea up the River Ness in the last 10,000 years. On top of that, since plesiosaurs are supposed to be cold-blooded, there's no way they could have survived the freezing Loch Ness waters.

Some speculate that it's more likely that the monster is a primitive whale, an archetype with a neck like a serpent's. It's thought that this creature has been extinct for the past 18 million years. Skeptics say that what people were calling the Loch Ness monster were just seiches. Seiches are oscillations caused by the inflow of the river's cold water onto the warmer waters of the loch, and they show up on the surface of the water.

Despite what skeptics thought, people continued to seek out this monster. In fact, many reporters were sent to Scotland from Britain, including reporters from the *Daily Mail*, who hired a big-game hunter named Marmaduke Wetherell. Marmaduke had found footprints that belonged to a four-legged creature of epic proportions. This discovery prompted the *Daily Mail of London* to put out a headline that read, "MONSTER OF LOCH NESS IS NOT LEGEND BUT A FACT." Of course, this fueled the mania around the Nessie.

Tons of tourists came to Loch Ness and would sit on deck chairs or boats waiting to see the beast. The footprints were cast in plaster and then sent over to the British Natural History Museum. It was found that the tracks belonged to a hippopotamus that was probably stuffed, not the mysterious monster everyone hoped they'd find. This caused the mania around the Loch Ness creature to die down a bit. Still, ever since then, many have claimed to have seen the Loch Ness monster, but many of those sightings have been hoaxes.

This monster dwells in Loch Ness, a large body of fresh water close to Inverness, Scotland. While this beast is said to have dwelled in the lake as far back as 1,600 years, there's no indisputable evidence of it yet. However, people continue to report sightings, and the public continues to go crazy over the Nessie. One of the earliest records of this monster comes from 500 AD, where local Picts carved an odd water creature close to Loch Ness.

Then there's the record of the monster from the Saint Columba biography from the 7th century. The biographer claims that Saint Columba was headed to see the ruler of the northern Picts close to Inverness. He had to stop at Loch Ness to deal with a beast that killed anyone who entered the lake. He spotted the large beast getting ready to attack someone else, and he stepped in to stop it by invoking God's name and commanding the beast to return with haste to where it came from. The beast was compelled to obey him and never hurt anyone else again.

Hoax or not, it doesn't look like the hunt for this monster will end anytime soon. Even before that infamous photograph, this monster was revered in water magic and still is today. If you want to, you can call on it when you want to amplify the power of your spells. Invoke the Nessie when you want to work spells regarding remaining invisible or unnoticed by people and institutions you'd rather not have sticking their noses in your business.

The Ghost of Piper of Clanyard Bay

In Scotland, it's hard not to recognize the blast of bagpipes. There are many stories about ghost pipers in Scottish lore. A maze of dark tunnels extends from the cliffs of Clanyard Bay to Grennan Cove. According to locals, the Fae dwelled in these caves and tunnels, so no one would ever dare to go in and bother them. One day though, a piper dared to go in, playing his pipes loudly as well. His loyal dog followed him. On and on, the music droned for hours, fading away slowly until no one could hear it anymore. Then the dog suddenly dashed out of the cave, howling in terror and completely hairless. As for the piper, no one saw him ever again.

While the caves no longer exist, it is said that passersby can still hear the distant sound of the bagpipes on summer nights coming from underground. Is it simply the sound of the wind as it whistles through the subterranean caves? Or is it just the mind playing tricks? Or could it very well be that the ghost of the piper is doomed to play his bagpipe for all eternity? No one knows for sure.

Selkies

The selkies can transform themselves into humans and then back into seals. This legend comes from the Shetland and Orkney Islands. The word selk or selch is Scottish for "seal."

There are stories aplenty about a man who had stumbled upon a beautiful female selkie on the beach as she was sunbathing. He decided he would steal her skin, and then he forced her to marry him and have his kids. The selkie woman is usually depicted staring out at the ocean with love in her eyes because she yearns to return home.

So many years later, she found her skin and escaped from the man. She became a seal again and headed back to the sea, turning her back on her abductor and her kids and never returning. Some say that she does return to see her kids once a year, while others claim that children see a large seal coming towards them to say hello when they're on the beach.

There's another version of the legend from Shetland from 1822. It says the selkie was already married to her own kind in the sea before she was forcefully abducted and made to remain on the land. Some tales from Shetland claim that selkies lure islanders to the sea each midsummer, and those who follow never return to land.

The StoorWorm

Also known as the Mester StoorWorm, this is a giant sea serpent from Orcadian folklore. It could destroy animals and people with its horrific, putrid breath and contaminate and poison plants. This is likely an Orkney spin on the Norse Jormungandr, also called the world serpent or the Midgard Serpent, and is described as resembling a sea dragon.

Each Saturday, as the sun rises, the Mester StoorWorm rises as well, opening its gigantic mouth and yawning nine times. Next, the creature demands that he be fed a breakfast of seven virgins. The old stories stated that as venomous and huge as he was, his taste was rather "dainty."

A country's king found that the beast was a threat. His advisors told him to give it a sacrifice of seven virgins each week. Desperate, the king sent word around the kingdom that he was offering his daughter for marriage as well as a magical sword for whoever was brave and powerful enough to slay the beast.

Assipattle was the son of a local farmer and the youngest one at that. He took on the challenge and defeated the monster. As it died, all its teeth fell out of its mouth and became the Faroes, Shetland, and Orkney islands. As for its body, it became Iceland.

One interesting thing to note about the slaying of this beast is that many other stories sound remarkably similar. It's theorized that the similarities are because the stories came to be at a point in time when enlightenment was born. At this time, making human sacrifices to monsters and other mythical beasts was becoming an archaic practice.

Say, for instance, that someone or something is causing you major grief in your life. You want to get rid of them, so you decide to work some banishing water magic. You can craft an incantation or a spell based on this story. Hold this intention: as Assipattle vanquished the Mester StoorWorm, so shall the situation or person be removed from your life and reduced to nothing. You could also draw on the power of Assipattle himself.

Robert the Bruce and the Spider

Most Scottish people know about Robert the Bruce and his part in the Scottish independence ward depicted in movies like Outlaw King. Born at Lochmaben Castle in 1274, Annandale's Knight and Overlord, Robert the Bruce, was crowned Scotland's king in 1306. He tried valiantly to set the country free from their enemies, the English. When the Earl of Pembroke defeated him in battle at Methven in 1306, Robert the Bruce hid in the Western Isles, dwelling in a cave for three months. He had hit rock bottom and was trying to figure out his next course of action. He thought about simply leaving Scotland and never coming back.

However, as he waited in the cave, it is said that he watched a spider construct a web at the cave's mouth. Scottish weather is always stormy, making it very hard for the spider to build its web. Whatever progress the spider made would be destroyed by water droplets. Still, the spider persevered, and eventually, it completed the web.

So inspired was Robert the Bruce by the spider's valiant efforts and persistence that he decided if a spider could keep going against the odds, then he could too. So, he picked himself up again and decided to fight. He reportedly told his men the popular saying, "If at first, you don't succeed, try, try, and try again." This is a saying that we still use even to this day. You can use this story to create water spells to give you persistence, perseverance, and success against all odds.

Chapter Eight: Water Meditation and Divination

If you want to become a spiritual powerhouse, you should consider practicing water meditation. Water is a cleansing and purifying element, so when you meditate close to a waterfall, lake, river, or sea, you will feel your mind become calmer and clearer. Water represents peace and purity, so it only makes sense that water meditation would put your mind, body, and spirit at ease.

Meditation is excellent for boosting your mental health. It can strengthen you mentally and emotionally. There are many ways to meditate, and one of the most powerful forms of this practice is water meditation. There's nothing quite like being deeply focused on the here and now, feeling the energy of water as it moves.

You might be quite surprised by the various methods by which you can meditate with water. The only limit is your imagination. If you've never been able to go deep in your meditation, you should definitely consider meditating with water. Not only will it help you focus, but you'll also become in tune with the energy of this element. That means you will be able to draw on or channel its power when you're working magic or just setting intentions, even when there's no water close to you. Water meditation is a joyful practice that makes you feel clean and at peace.

What Water Represents in Meditation

Water gives purity. If you want to clean your home, car, clothes, or body, you need water; there's no way around it. If you want to flush out impurities from your system, it makes sense to up your water intake as it helps your body clean itself thoroughly. Water is the ultimate cleanser. So, as you meditate, you can see all worries, concerns, and ugly energy as dirt. Envision yourself being cleansed by water. See it as rainfall that washes away the dust and dirt from your life, allowing you to feel new and clean again.

Water brings clarity. When you have a drink of water, think about how refreshed you feel. Also, consider the very appearance of water. In its truest form, it is clean and clear. You can see through it to whatever lies at the bottom. There's nothing in the water that can be hidden from you. Think about this as you meditate with water. If there are matters in your life that confuse you or things you feel are being hidden from you, contemplate the purity and clarity of the water. Intend that, just as water is crystal clear, so is the solution to the problem you have, and the secrets that are kept from you become very clear to see.

Water gives calmness. This is especially true when you consider the sound of water. Think about the pitter-patter of raindrops as they fall onto the earth. Alternatively, recall the sound of the ocean's waves, rushing in, rolling back out. Think about the powerful sound of waterfalls, the unspeakable potency that lies in storms. Think of the steady sound of dripping water from a tap. Imagine it's dripping in a cave, and the sound bounces and echoes magically all around you. Imagine the sound of a brook or a stream as it gently flows on its way, lapping around rocks and twigs. The next time you pour water into a glass, listen to the beautiful sound it makes. Whether it's being poured, is flowing, or dripping, water moves with ease, peace, and grace, and this sound can also cause you to feel a sense of calm. You can also intend that as the sound of water puts one at ease, so do you make others feel relaxed when they're in your space.

Water Meditation Methods

One way to meditate with water is to be around water, whether it's a pond, river, or lake. If you can't get to a body of water, you can simply meditate in your bathtub as you take a bath or shower. You can even work with a bottle or cup of water if that's all you can manage. You'd have to hold the water in your hands, and when you're done meditating, you can drink it. When there's no water around you, you can simply visualize your preferred body of water or bring the sound of moving water to your mind as you meditate.

Using Your Thoughts

What do you do when there's no water around you? To quote a purple dinosaur, "Just use your imagination." Here's what you need to do:

1. Find a space that is comfortable, quiet, and free from any distraction. You want to make sure no one will bother you for at least 10 to 15 minutes.

2. Make sure you're wearing loose, comfortable clothing and that you're nice and warm.

3. Sit on the floor in lotus or on a chair if you prefer. Whatever position works for you is fine, as long as you can remain in it comfortably for the duration of the meditation.

4. Place your hands on your lap, keeping your shoulders and neck relaxed. Close your eyes, and part your lips slightly. Make sure your jaw is relaxed.

5. Take a deep breath. Inhale through your nose, allowing both your belly and your chest to rise as the air fills your lungs.

6. Hold that breath for just a couple of seconds, and then allow it all to come out through your slightly parted lips. You might notice the exhale is longer than the inhale; this is completely fine.

7. Continue to breathe in and out this way until you notice your body and mind relaxing.

8. If you notice your mind wandering away from your breath (and it will), don't be mad. Instead, be glad you noticed it, and gently, lovingly return your attention to your breath. If you're new to meditation, you may get distracted easily and frequently. Whatever you do, don't beat yourself up for it. It's natural, and it's always good to notice because, with time, you'll get distracted less and less.

9. As you relax into your breath, allow your mind to become aware of your body and the floor.

10. Gradually let your awareness of the floor and your body drift into nothing. Do this as you continue to breathe in and out.

11. Feel your eyelids get heavier and heavier as you breathe.

12. See yourself as water, pure, clean, and calm in your mind's eye.

13. Imagine you're being poured into a bowl. Think about how it feels. Are you calm? Do you feel like you're moving around? Do you feel cold or warm?

14. Realize in your heart that you are water. Accept that you are clarity, purity, and calmness. Allow yourself to be washed over by these feelings, and lose yourself in water.

15. Notice what you feel in the moment.

16. Now, envision yourself cleaning a dirty thing that represents whatever troubles you are faced with in life. Notice the way the dirt yields to you and runs off the object into nothingness. Notice how it becomes clean and whole as you run over and through it.

17. Feel your cleansing power, too strong for anything or anyone impure to withstand. Embody this feeling and revel in it.

18. When you're ready to end your session, return your attention to your breath.

19. Allow your consciousness to return to your body slowly. Feel the ground beneath you and the room around you with your eyes still shut.

20. Take one last cleansing breath, and then open your eyes.

Working with Water Bodies

Now let's go over how to work with bodies of water that you can find around you.

Still Water: This sort of water reflects whatever hovers above it. You can work with a kiddy pool or just a bowl of water. Look into the water and take note of the reflections you see. Notice the way your surroundings seem to blend with the water. Touch it and see how still and calm it is. Use your hands to move the water about, troubling it, and notice the way you feel about that. Pay attention to the way the water eventually settles down and becomes still again. Move the water about with your hand again. This time imagine that all that chaos is whatever you're dealing with in life that's causing you grief. Then stop moving the water about, and as the water settles again, imagine that every bothersome situation in your life settles just the same way.

Rippling Water: You can find this sort of water in calm rivers or fountains. If you prefer, you can cast pebbles into a pond or lake to create your own ripples. As you toss the stones, notice the way they skip across the water. Think about what that reminds you of and how the stone and water interact with each other. Think about how the stone can escape the water's grasp time and time again but is always eventually claimed by the water.

Now, think about a situation in your life that you're having trouble finding a solution for. You know there's an answer, but it always seems to evade you. Now, imagine that situation is the pebble, and you're the water. As you cast the pebble, and it pops out of the water for the last time, imagine you're the water that has finally overcome whatever you're dealing with. If you're working with water that ripples on its own, you can envision what it's like to be right in the middle of those ripples. How does it feel to simply flow? Imagine that just as the ripples move effortlessly and gracefully, you live your life every day the same way.

Moving Water: You can work with a stream if you want moving water. Contemplate the speed at which it moves. Is it fast or slow? Notice the way it meanders around rocks and corners. Notice how no matter what's in its way, it continues to push on. Think about the fact that the gentle moving water may encounter an obstacle. Still, as it continues to move, it inevitably wears it down. If there's a jagged rock along its path, think about the fact that with time, the graceful water will smoothen it out completely. Consider the jagged aspects of your life that cause you pain or discontent. Think of yourself as water, continuing to move on with your life despite the jagged edges. Imagine that you gracefully smooth over whatever it is you're dealing with, proving that in the end, the power has always been within you.

Rushing Water: You can work with the sea or a waterfall or any body of water that rushes rapidly with a strong current. See this powerful force of nature, moving relentlessly. Consider how it could never possibly be stopped, no matter what one does. Pay attention to the sound of the water as it rushes. Feel its power. Imagine that this water undoes everything in your life that's holding you back. Envision it as it moves relentlessly. Watch it eroding all things that no longer serve you in your life, leaving you light, clean, and free to be the grandest version of yourself. Shut your eyes and feel the raw power of the water through its vibrations. That power is unmistakable. Whenever you feel afraid or are faced with a situation you feel is beyond your ability to handle, remember the powerful vibrations of the rushing water. Understand that the same power in the water is alive and thrives within your soul. You can access this power whenever you want, and everyone and everything in your path has no choice but to kowtow to your will.

Water Scrying

Water is an excellent medium for scrying. You can divine the future by working with water. More than just seeing the future, you can gain knowledge about the past and the present. You can also discover secrets, find things you thought were forever lost, and become aware of the energies that influence situations and people. Some people choose to use tarot, runes, or bones to do this. Water scrying is another good method to use. It's different in that you have to keep your attention focused on the scrying object. While some scryers use mirrors, crystal balls, or other reflective surfaces, others use water. With enough focus and time, you'll begin to notice images on the water's surface. You might see a simple thing like smoke in motion or an entire scene acted out before you, as shown on television.

The best sort of water to work with when scrying is still water. You can work with cups, chalices, basins, or bowls. You could even scry with a puddle. There are also herbal tinctures meant to improve your scrying results, but you don't have to use those if you don't have them or want to.

How Water Scrying Works

Scrying depends on the Ganzfeld effect. The word *Ganzfeld* is German and means "entire field," referring to your field of vision. When your eyes haven't had access to stimuli for a while, your brain will begin to seek some visual input. When it can't find anything to pick up on, it will blow up the neural noise in your head to give it something to focus on. When you're not actually scrying, this can create hallucinations. However, scrying is a different ballgame from seeing what isn't there. It's beyond mere hallucinations. Your job is to find specific information and symbols and to interpret them from a divinatory standpoint.

Let me put this another way: scrying relies on you having a visual field with little or no stimuli so you can focus on the messages you'll receive from the spirit realm on the scrying medium, which, in this case, is water. The process of your brain seeking visual input can be manipulated to let you enter a different state of consciousness where you can access divinatory messages.

Some water scryers don't work with visuals. As water transmits information and vibrations, some scryers will use their bowls to learn what they need using just sound. It's the equivalent of someone using their fingertips to play sounds on the rims of wine glasses. The rubbing motion causes the glass to give off a note. Here, the diviner will add water that they usually collect on a full moon and then use that water to moisten their wand or fingertips. Then they'll strike the bowl's rim and interpret the messages from the hum they produce.

You can scry whenever you like, but if you're having difficulty connecting with water, you should try to scry on a full moon. You should also gather the scrying water on a full moon. If you can't, you can just put some clean water in a bowl and put it out under the moonlight. Let it sit there till right before the sun rises. Make sure you change this water regularly so it doesn't grow stagnant.

What You Need to Water Scry

- A bowl (usually opaque black)

- Freshwater (make it from a natural source if you can)

- A candle

Lighting a candle and setting it right outside your visual field will put you in an even better position to switch your consciousness to the spirit world. If you're scrying with harmonics instead, you will need a wand made of hazel or laurel. Keep in mind that the first few tries will likely disappoint you. There's nothing wrong with that. The point of practicing those times is to become comfortable with the process. With time, you'll begin to scry successfully.

How to Water Scry

1. First, be clear on your intention. What question do you want answers to? What is your goal? Be clear about it.

2. Sit somewhere you won't be disturbed, and let your water be just a foot before you.

3. If possible, make sure there are no surfaces that give off a glare or reflect onto the water you're working with. It helps to dim the lights, and if you want to, work with a candle. Make sure the candle is somewhere safe. Since the candle will be out of your field of vision, the last thing you need is to worry about whether the open flame may start a fire.

4. Allow your body to relax. Unclench your jaw, lower your shoulders, and breathe easily.

5. Let your eyes go close halfway, allowing your gaze to drop to the water's surface. Don't try to force yourself to see something, and don't stare too hard. Just keep your gaze natural and easy.

6. When the Ganzfeld effect kicks in, you will notice your vision start to blackout from the edges. The blackness will move toward the middle, but don't panic – this is normal. Your brain is simply turning its attention from your actual vision to your more subtle senses.

7. Next, you may begin to see colors and shapes on the water surface. For most people, it begins as a little speck that balloons into a smoke cloud.

8. If you feel you need to blink, go ahead. Note that blinking will interrupt the Ganzfeld effect, but there's nothing wrong with that. The last thing you want to do is beat up on yourself out of frustration; this won't help you get results or help you get better at your practice. *You should relax and start afresh.* Relaxation during your scrying will give you great results, and the more you practice this, the better you'll get and the easier it will be.

9. Suppose you can only see colors and smoke. Attempt to work out what they mean. What do the colors mean to you? How might they be related to your question? If it's smoke, think about what its movement might be. When the smoke moves to the right, it's interpreted as a "yes." When it blows to the left, it means "no." Take note of everything you see and what it all means to you each time you scry.

You need to remember that your divination ability is like a muscle. The more you use it, the stronger it becomes. So don't quit, and continue to track all you see each time you scry. Make it a habit, and you will soon begin to get very clear answers. Don't put pressure or a time limit on yourself. If you have spent about fifteen minutes and haven't seen anything, you can stop and try again later that day or the next. The clarity will come with time and practice.

Chapter Nine: Ten Water Spells to Know

Water spells are amazingly powerful, and it's awesome to know that you can find water almost everywhere you go. It's in the ground, the sky, the air, the food you eat, and even when you can't see water for miles like in the desert, it's in you. You can work with the snow or the sea, ice or steam, whatever you want. As a water magician, you should spend time each day expressing your gratitude for this wonderful element. Become more mindful of water, and your bond with it will improve, as well as your ability to wield its magic in your craft.

You don't have to make a big show of appreciating water. You can simply say thank you each time you drink it, shower with it, or come in contact with it in any way. The more you do this, the more you will feel its power and presence in your life. You will receive many blessings because you've chosen to be grateful for this life-giving gift made so freely available to all. You must always be sincere with your gratitude. Don't just say it mindlessly, only looking to get something in return. Develop a relationship with water.

The more common water spells involve washing, diluting, and putting things or one's self into water. The magic of this element is so strong that even the rise of Christianity could do little to destroy its historical roots. So, it was incorporated into the religion. You can tell from the practice of baptism and using holy water to heal, bless, and exorcise demons.

You can perform water spells wherever you are. Still, you'll have the absolute best results when you're as close to a natural water source as possible - bonus points if it's a source of water you resonate with deeply. However, don't be disappointed if you can't easily access a natural water source. Water is so powerful that it will work for you regardless of its form, as long as you are very clear about your intention. You should not doubt that you will receive the answers and manifestations you seek.

Spells for Protection

The Minty Purge

You'll Need

- 2 bowls

- Non-iodized sea salt (regular sea salt will also do in a pinch)

- Dried or fresh mint (or parsley)

- Water

Steps

1. Put water into one bowl and a little bit of salt in another. Set both bowls in front of you along with your sprig of parsley or mint.

2. Cast a circle of protection around yourself. It doesn't matter if you're indoors or outdoors, but if the latter is the case, you can use a stick to draw a circle around yourself in the soft dirt close to the body of water.

3. If you want to, you can place eight stones around the circle. Alternatively, you can place eight pinches of salt around the circle. Follow your intuition here. If you're

leaning towards using crystals, shells, or herbs, you can do that. Make sure the circle is around you and the magical items.

4. Shut your eyes and envision a bright white light springing from the circle in the ground, surrounding you and shielding you.

5. In your mind's eye, see yourself in a wide-open field that is full of loving energy and has no negative energy. If you'd rather imagine yourself somewhere else that you feel safe, protected, and loved, you can do that. It doesn't matter what imagery you go for, as long as you generate a feeling of calm, safety, and protection. You want to be very clear about your intention to be protected and make sure your thoughts and emotions about being safe are unmistakable. Truly believe that you're safe before you carry on with the next step.

6. Hold the bowl of water and allow your eyelids to drop down to half-mast. Gaze into it easily, and allow your mind to travel to any negative energy or worry that may come up.

7. When you feel negative emotions, gently say: "There's no need to be alarmed by what dares to cause me harm. For this water keeps me safe and banishes evil away."

8. Gently and firmly banish the thought that showed up in your mind, and allow the negative energy to move from you into the water. Consider it banished.

9. Now it's time to purify the water. Put the water bowl down and add a pinch of salt.

10. You can repeat the process two times or more if you notice that fearful thoughts keep coming up. Continue to purge them into the water and then purify it with salt.

11. When you're finally at peace, take the mint or parsley and soak it in the saltwater. You should hold it so that your fingers won't touch the water and pick up on the negative energy. The herb will absorb that negativity.

12. Make sure you're not touching the wet part of the herb, bury it in the ground, and then say, "Dearest mint (or parsley), I thank you most profusely. For there is not even a hint of danger drawn unto me."

13. You're done with this spell. Wash the bowl carefully with fresh water that has salt in it.

Protected by Four Thieves

The main ingredient is Vinegar Marseilles or Four Thieves Vinegar. It has been used for many centuries in protection and healing spells. You should formulate this when the moon is waning so that all influences you do not desire will easily leave you alone, and you'll be safe.

You'll Need

- 1 large glass bottle or jar
- ½ cup apple cider vinegar
- 1 cup spring water
- 3 drops thyme oil
- 3 drops clove oil
- 3 drops lavender oil
- 3 drops common sage oil

Steps

1. Set all the ingredients on your altar.

2. Put the vinegar and the water into your bottle or jar.

3. Add your oils, and then close the bottle firmly.

4. Give the bottle a nice shake so that all the ingredients blend nicely.

5. Loosen the cap a bit, and then set the mix out on your windowsill or in your yard for the sun's rays to charge it.

6. Leave it there when the waning moon is out so that it can absorb the moonlight energy as well.

7. It is now complete. Put 2 to 3 tablespoons into a bathtub full of water. Have this bath as needed over the next 7 days. If anything is left of this mixture after a week, please discard it. Make a fresh batch if you need to.

High John the Conqueror Protective Bath

You'll Need

- 1 High John root (small, grated)
- 1 jar or bottle
- ¼ cup holy water
- ½ cup spring water
- 6 drops lemon oil
- 6 drops lime oil
- 6 drops vetiver oil
- 6 drops of bergamot oil

Steps

1. Place all ingredients on your altar.

2. Fill your jar with the holy water and spring water.

3. Add the grated High John root with the lemon, lime, vetiver, and bergamot oils.

4. Cover the jar or bottle securely, then shake it thoroughly, infusing it with the intention that the user is safe and protected at all times and in all ways.

5. Next, rub the bottle in between your hands over and over, quickly as you can, to charge it with even more protective intention and energy. You can call on your preferred deity to lend their energy as well.

6. It's now ready for your use. Give it one more shake, and then add 2 large tablespoons of the mixture into a tub full of water. If you think you might clog your tub, then you should strain the mixture with a cheesecloth.

7. Have this bath each night till the mixture is finished.

Spells for Love

Love Drawing Spell

This spell is great for when you want to draw a lover to you. Please only use this if you're single, searching, and ready for the responsibility that comes with being in a relationship with someone.

You'll Need

- Glass bottle (small)
- Sandalwood oil (3 drops)
- Thyme oil (3 drops)
- 3 apple seeds
- Sweet almond oil (¼ ounce)

Steps

1. Place all these ingredients on your shrine or altar.

2. Put the sweet almond oil into the glass bottle.

3. Add your sandalwood and thyme oils.

4. Toss in the apple seeds.

5. Cover the bottle properly.

6. Toss the bottled up in the air gently, and then catch it. By doing this, you've sent the bottle magically and metaphorically into the realm of spirit, and spirit has blessed it.

7. Carry out a little patch test on your skin with the oil mixture to ensure you won't react to it badly.

8. Put a bit of this oil on the back of your neck. Also, apply some to the soles of your feet and your wrists. Do this before you go to bed.

9. Make sure you have a pen and paper close to you so you can write down your dreams once you wake up.

10. If you aren't adept at connecting to the dream world yet, don't worry. Constantly writing down your dreams will help you. In the meantime, you can repeat this spell several more times till you finally receive a vision of your lover.

Love Thyme Bath

If you want to have a lovely, passionate night with your significant other, then this is the spell for you. It will help you make your deepest wishes come true, and you and your partner will have an even stronger bond than ever before. You'll also notice that you're more eager to connect with each other physically.

You'll Need

- 1 large saucepan
- 2 cups tap water
- 2 cups spring water
- ½ cup passionflower blossoms (dried)
- ½ cup rose petals (dried)
- ½ cup thyme leaves (dried)
- 1 large glass jar or bottle

- A cheesecloth

Steps

1. Heat the waters on your stove using medium heat.

2. When the water starts to simmer, take it off the heat and add your rose, thyme, and passionflower.

3. Allow this mix to stand until it cools down or for an hour.

4. Strain the mix with your cheesecloth.

5. Pour it into the jar or bottle, and cover it when it's full.

6. You can put some in a spray bottle and spritz it around your room and on yourself, or just take a bath with it. You can keep this for 7 days, but no longer.

The Gris-Gris of Love

Pronounced gree-gree, the gris-gris bag is just like a mojo bag. You can carry it around to get the results you seek. Carry it around till you experience the love you seek.

You'll Need

- 3 drops oil of ylang-ylang

- 3 drops oil of jasmine

- 1 teaspoon red rose petals (dried)

- 1 small rose quartz

- 1 small ceramic or glass bowl

- 1 mixing spoon

- 1 red small drawstring pouch (or a small piece of red cloth and a red string.

Steps

1. Set everything on your altar.

2. Put the oils and rose petals into your bowl and mix it all up by stirring clockwise till it's thoroughly blended.

3. Put this mix into the gris-gris bag. If you're using cloth instead, put the mix in the middle of it.

4. Put the rose crystal in the mix as well.

5. If you're using a cloth and string, gather the corners of the cloth together and tie them off securely with the string. If not, simply draw the string on your drawstring pouch tightly, ensuring all items are secure.

6. Rub this bag in your hands back and forth, and as you do, feel love, warmth, passion, and openness flowing from your heart and mind through your hands and into the bag.

7. Your bag is ready for use. Put it in your pocket and take it everywhere you go to bring love to you.

A Potent Healing Spell: Powder of Health

This spell works as a sprinkling powder that you can use in your home to help promote healing and health.

You'll Need

- 1 teaspoon thyme
- 1 teaspoon cinnamon
- 1 tablespoon black sat
- 1 mixing spoon
- 1 ceramic or glass bowl

Steps

1. Gather all these ingredients and mix them in your bowl with the spoon till they're thoroughly combined.

2. Pinch a bit of this mixture and then sprinkle it in the corners of each room in your home, moving in a clockwise direction. You can replace it after several weeks or when you sense you should.

Rice Money Magnet Magic

You can work as hard as you like and get results, but if you want to reap even better fruits from your labor, it does help to work some water magic.

You'll Need

- 1 bucket
- 1 glass jar
- Paper towels
- 3 drops green food coloring
- ½ cup jasmine rice 1 teaspoon gold glitter
- 1 tablespoon iron filings
- 1 tablespoon cinnamon powder
- 1 tablespoon holy water
- 3 drops green food coloring
- 6 drops cypress oil
- 1-quart spring water
- Shredded money bill (either $10 or higher)

Steps

1. Set all the items on your altar

2. Put the food coloring and holy water into the jar, cover it and give it a good shake.

3. Add the rice and stir the mix till it's well blended and uniformly colored.

4. Add the glitter, iron filings, cinnamon, and shredded money.

5. Cover the jar securely and give it another shake.

6. Spread out the rice on your paper towels and set it by a window that gets sunlight so that it can dry completely. This might take 1 or 2 days.

7. Put the rice back into the jar to store it.

8. For the floor wash, put the spring water into the bucket.

9. Add the cypress oil and stir till properly combined.

10. Add some of the money rice. You only need 3 tablespoons.

11. Your money wash is ready. You can use it to wipe down your office space, cash register, windows, floors, and your home if you work remotely. Also, use it to wipe down the tools of your trade.

Memory Spell: Solid Memory Gris-Gris

You'll Need

- 1 teaspoon five finger grass (dried)
- 1 teaspoon rosemary (dried)
- 1 strand of your hair
- 1 bay leaf (whole, dried)

- 1 azurite crystal (small)

- 1 ceramic or glass bowl

- 1 mixing spoon

- 1 small blue bag (make sure the material is natural)

Steps

1. Place all the ingredients on your altar.

2. Put the bowl in the middle of the altar and add your hair and the herbs.

3. Use the spoon to mix it thoroughly. Make sure you stir clockwise.

4. Put the mix into the blue bag.

5. Add the azurite crystal into the bag.

6. Let the bag remain on the windowsill where the sun rays and moonlight can charge it for 24 hours.

7. After this, it's ready for use. Take this around with you to help you remember things better.

Weather Magic: A Rain Drawing Spell

You'll Need

- 1 large glass bowl

- 1 rose of Jericho flower (dried)

- 1 cup spring water

- 1 cup rainwater

- 3 drops cypress oil

- 3 drops lavender oil

Steps

1. Set all items on your altar.

2. Put the rose of Jericho in the middle of your bowl.

3. Imagine the rain falling generously on the area you want to relieve from heat, drought, or raging fires, as you pour the oils and the waters into the bowl.

4. For three days and nights, allow the rose of Jericho to sit in the bowl. You can add more spring water as needed if you notice it's evaporating.

5. Take the rose of Jericho out of the bowl to your closet body of water, and then bury it in the soft earth close to it.

6. Turn around and head back home, following a different path. Don't look back.

Making Magical Waters

You can make your water spells even more powerful by working with magical water. Here's a quick guide on how to make various kinds of this water. Pro tip: Always label your waters immediately after bottling them up.

1. Moon Water: Put your preferred herbs into a bowl, fill it with water, and leave it where the moonlight can get to it. Allow it to remain there overnight and bottle it up before sunrise because you don't want the sun to get to it.

2. Sun Water: This is made the same way you make moon water. Leave it out in the sun and bring it in before the moonlight can touch it.

3. Storm Water: You can collect this from a thunderstorm. It's packed full of energy from the wind, thunder, lightning, and barometric pressure. You can also just put a jar of water by the windowsill when there's a lightning storm. Some witches work with tornado and hurricane water. Still, you need to beware that these are extremely potent, so only work your magic with them for good.

4. Snow Water: This is basically water from melted snow. You can use the first snow of the season and save it in a bottle to use it all through the year. Use it for magic meant to calm angry people down or bring peace to yourself.

5. Rose Water: This is water infused with roses. You can infuse roses into the water just using heat. Use it for love, protection, and improving psychic abilities. It also does wonders for headaches.

6. Florida Water: This isn't actually water. It's a blend of essential oils that have been mixed using a solvent. It is a powerful cleanser. You can have a bath with it during a New Moon to banish negativity. You can also use it to wash your floors and doors to attract blessings. It can be purchased from your local Walmart or superstore, which is simpler than making your own. Just make sure you bless it and infuse it with your own intentions and energy.

7. Holy Water: Generally, this is water blessed by a deeply spiritual person. In witchcraft, it's simply water you've charged with magical intention. Use this to cleanse yourself and your magical tools, as well as your space. To make it, just add some water into a bowl, add a pinch of salt, and envision the salt cleansing the water of all that's impure, physically and spiritually. Then draw a sacred symbol of power over the water bowl or jar, such as a rune, sacred geometry shame, triquetra, reiki symbol, infinity symbol, etc. You can draw this symbol with a finger or a wand if you have one. Draw it no less than three times and no more than nine times. As you draw the symbol, imagine the water is pure, living energy, full of the essence of Divinity. See it glow with radiant white light. Speak over the water, blessing it and thanking it. Bottle it up.

Chapter Ten: Water Magic Rituals

Let's take a look at what a standard pagan or Wiccan ritual looks like. To be clear, this is only a template. None of this is set in stone, and you can always make the rituals your own by adding elements that resonate with you or using your own spells and incantations.

Having a Standard Ritual

1. Figure out the ritual you want to perform. There are many Pagan and Wiccan rituals. You just need to find the one that suits your needs. A good one to look up is the Drawing down the Moon ritual.

2. Make a solid plan. Think about who will be around for the ritual, figure out who will preside over which quarter, lead what part of the ritual, etc. This planning is essential so that you don't find yourself confused in the middle of the practice and ruin the energy. It's also a sign of respect to the spirits you work with when you come prepared.

3. Prep the space. Will you be working the ritual outdoors or inside? If you're working outside, you need to make sure the space is free and clear of trash and that it's safe for the magicians joining you to move about barefoot if they decide to. Also, you need to select an appropriate spot where you won't be distracted or attract unwanted attention. Think about how you'll set up your magical tools as well. If you're working inside, make sure you smudge or sweep the ritual space before and after you're all done to get rid of unwanted energy.

4. Cleanse and purify yourself. You can take a shower or a bath with cleansing water, salts, and oils that correspond with the ritual you'll be partaking in.

5. Center yourself. Be in the moment. Forget about your worries and regrets and just focus on the now. Make sure there are no distractions. Close your eyes and breathe, and focus on why you're all gathered there.

6. Cast your circle. You should have already cleansed the space by now, so you need to gather the group in a circle and then cast a circle around everyone. You can walk around the participants clockwise as you sprinkle salt on the floor or use other elements like crystals, herbs, shells, and so on to create the circle. Ensure that every magical object and offering for the ritual is within the circle as well. If you're working indoors and hosting a large gathering, you could cast a circle around your home once everyone is in. Also, note that you and your altar should face the north as you finish your ritual. To complete the circle, you need to set candles or other sacred items at each cardinal point. If you're using candles, don't light them just yet. You might want to use something to represent the elements of Earth in the north, fire in the south, the air in the east, and water in the west. Then, walk around the circle, lighting your candles as you trail salt around its circumference.

7. Take some time to honor the gods and goddesses with whom you'll be working. It helps if you have a symbolic sculpture or image of them, particularly for group rituals, so that you can all maintain your focus on the same thing. If you like, you can choose to chant the name of the being you will work with.

8. Visualize your intention and take time to meditate on it. Do this before you cast your spell.

9. Offer thanks to your sacred deities who helped you with this ritual. Not only will they keep you safe, but they also hear your prayer and do all in their power to make things work out for your benefit.

10. Thank the elements as well and release each one in reverse order. You have to do this to let go of all remaining energy.

11. Ground yourself in the present moment. You can do this by hugging one another, eating something, or touching your body all over so you can become more aware of the physical. You can also imagine roots are growing out of your feet that connect you to the Earth, steadying and grounding you.

12. Whether a group ritual or a solitary one, you can have some cake and wine as part of the blessing and grounding. Pass the wine first, and then the cake. Do so in a clockwise motion, with each person blessing the drink and food before having some and passing it to someone else.

13. Discuss any insights you gained during the ritual. Some people may have received visions or flashes of inspiration that could help someone - or everyone - present. So, it's often a good idea to share these experiences.

When done, write your experiences and observations in your grimoire. Your grimoire is where you write down every experience you have with your magical ritual. You should also write down spells, recipes for potions, powders, washes, and any insight that you glean from your rituals and meditations. The insight you write down may have come directly from you or someone else in the group. Either way, all that matters is that it rings true to you.

Purification Rituals

Some religions observe ablutions, also called ritual washing. For instance, Judaism believes that ablutions must be performed religiously to become pure so that practitioners will bathe their bodies in a bath for ritual immersion, known as a *mikveh.* They'll also perform the netilat yadayim, where they wash their hands once they wake up and before every meal.

In Islam, they practice *wudu,* which is meant to keep one clean for daily prayers. In Christianity, baptism is of significant symbolic importance, as this is how one's soul is sanctified. In Hinduism, bathing yourself with sacred water removes all spiritual impurities from your soul. It will help to set you free from the cycle of life and death called Moksha.

You can turn your regular shower or bath into a purification ritual as well. Simply adding salt to the mix and declaring yourself purified in mind, body, and soul is more than enough to cleanse you, as long as your intention is clear, strong, and pure.

Water Drinking Rituals

When next you have a glass or bottle of water in your hand, close your eyes for a moment. Feel deep and sincere appreciation for the water you have in your hand. Allow this water to connect you to the seas, rivers, streams, rains, storms, tornadoes, and waterfalls. Allow this power to vibrate through the glass and your palms and into your heart. Then feel this energy radiate from your heart to every part of your body. As you drink this water, let yourself be filled with light and love, and notice how much more refreshed you feel than if you'd simply taken a thoughtless gulp of water.

Infusing Water with Prayer

When you're about to go to sleep, take a minute or two to write an affirmation or prayer that means a lot to you on a piece of paper. Take that paper and wrap it around your glass or bottle. As you wrap it, imagine that the water draws in the vibration and energy of your intentions and written words. Come morning, don't just gulp the water. Take a minute or two to sit with your intention and reconnect with the affirmation you wrote down. Sip on this water all through your day. Make each sip mindful by recalling the affirmation and prayer you made. Trust that it is done. Your desire will manifest on the physical plane at the right place and time, for the good of all.

Bathing and Washing Rituals

Daily washing gives you a chance to connect with water and its purifying energy. As you take a bath, declare aloud or intend in your heart that just as water cleanses you of all dirt, so are your mind, body, and soul cleansed from all negative and impure energies. Declare that as the water runs over your body, you are cleansed physically, emotionally, and spiritually.

Since you're washing away negativity and bad vibes you may have picked up from others over the day, you should wash your body with motions away from yourself. Take your time with each part of your body. Wash from the crown of your head to the soles of your feet. If you were taking a blessing or an attraction bath, you would work from your feet to your head and use motions toward yourself to scrub yourself clean.

It's so important to spiritually cleanse yourself each day or at least once a week. Say you perform rituals or pray for miracles. Your prayer was heard and answered, but you're so spiritually bogged down by the dirt of negativity and even malicious entities that you can't receive the blessings. Whatever good that should come your way will pass you by instead.

You'll notice this in your daily life, as things that should work out for you just don't, or they fail at the last minute. Cleansing yourself will banish all the negative energies keeping your success at bay. After cleansing yourself, when you perform other rituals for love, money, health, or anything else, you'll find that your manifestations are a lot faster and are more certain. So, make it a habit to perform cleansing rituals regularly.

Sacred immersion is a ritual that involves purifying and rejuvenating yourself. It has elements of Ayurveda along with other sacred rituals. You can use this immersion to bring calm to your mind, strengthen your heart, and keep your spirit pure. To do this, you'll need:

- A bathtub

- Incense (To invite the appropriate energy in your space)

- Natural massage oil

- Music (You can use chants or prayer songs to keep your mind clear and focused)

- Candles (To create a peaceful atmosphere. Use blue or white candles)

- Offerings

Your offerings are meant to be infused in your bath. They could be flowers like chamomile, pansies, roses, or dandelions. Essential oils like jasmine, geranium, lavender, rose oil, oats, milk, honey, and other natural ingredients will purify and soothe you.

Steps

1. Begin by filling your tub with water that's nice and warm.

2. Put the offerings close to the tub.

3. Light your candles and incense.

4. Put on your preferred music.

5. Close your eyes and begin to chant a mantra or just say a quick prayer.

6. One by one, add the offerings into the bath. Make sure you're intentional about it, feeling gratitude for each one and what it does for you.

7. Slowly get into the tub, fully aware of every sensation all over your body as you get into the warm water.

8. When you're fully immersed, take your time as you wash your body and bless each part.

9. Lie back in the tub and just meditate. Focus on your breath, or listen to the music, or keep up your chanting.

10. When you feel finished, you can get out of the bath and dry yourself off.

11. Use the oil to massage your body all over, blessing every part you touch.

12. For a moment, be still. Allow your heart to be filled with gratitude for the wonderful element of water and how it purifies you. Feel thankful that you could perform this act of self-love.

13. Unplug your drain. If you like, you can watch the water rush down your drain, knowing that it is carrying away everything impure to transform it into purity once more.

Purified by Living Water

It is important to acknowledge how sacred water is in Hinduism, especially water from natural sources like springs and rivers. This is a ritual based on Hindu beliefs, where you will work with natural waters, as they are inherently holy with no need for blessings.

Steps

1.Pick a spot. You might have to travel out of state if you're not fortunate enough to have a natural water source near your home. Either way, go somewhere with natural water that inspires you and gives you a sense of connection to the divine. Think about the way you intend to connect with the element. If you plan to immerse yourself, ensure you pick a safe spot for swimming or bathing.

2.Prep your prayers and offerings. You can take actual offerings along with you to the water. Make sure that they are all-natural and won't have a horrible effect on nature. You can take offerings like leaves, stones, flowers, and even rice. If you're taking food offerings, please be absolutely sure that it won't affect the wildlife negatively. You can also offer incense. As for your prayer, know that it's a personal thing. You can prepare a prayer that suits your intentions, or you can work with popular mantras or affirmations that you're drawn to.

3.Now it's time for the ceremony. You're going to set out your offerings and other things close to the water. Light your incense, and take a seat by the water's edge. Take a moment to feel the energy of the environment.

4.Chant a mantra or say your prayer in your mind or aloud, then release your offerings. If you're remaining on the shore, you can just put your offerings close to or into the water. If you're going to immerse yourself, then you should hold your offering at chest level, close to your heart, and then release it when you've gotten where you want to stop in the water. You can completely submerge your body beneath the water thrice, or you can cup some water in your hands and pour it over your head three times.

5.Each time you dip below the surface of the water or pour it over your head, envision the water cleansing your mind, spirit, and body. You can imagine that all the challenges you're facing at the moment are letting go of you each time you submerge yourself or pour water over your head.

6.Head back to the water's edge and sit in silent contemplation. Feel honored that water has and will continue to help you be the best version of yourself. Be grateful for how blessed and clean you now are.

7.Thank the water. You can also say your prayer again or recite the mantra.

Water is a wonderful life-saver and life-giver. It's vital for every creature on this little blue dot. There will never be a moment when this element will prove useless. There could never be a better substitute for it. It's no wonder that cultures worldwide always have revered water and that people innately know and understand its ability to purify and bless us all. Thanks to water, we are connected to all of life. We can connect with the power of water by working with water rituals and making it a routine.

Speaking of routines, it's so easy to fall into a trap where you mindlessly go through the motions and say all the right words because you've done them a thousand times before. So, I must warn you against that. Let every water ritual, spell, or enchantment you cast be a brand-new experience to you each time. Be very intentional about your words and actions, and understand why you're doing what you do. You're working with the element that keeps us all alive, so you should respect the vast power that water makes freely available to you.

Conclusion

Magically speaking, water is a lovely element that can bring you solutions to whatever problems you face. The more you practice water magic, the more aware you'll become of the hidden force that lies in this often-overlooked gift. A significant part of you is made up of water, and that, in turn, makes you magical. If you've never thought of yourself in that way before, practicing magic with this element will reveal the truth about yourself to you.

Sure, you're human, and humans are messy creatures. Sometimes we go looking for trouble, create quite a mess, and act like someone else needs to fix it. Sometimes we make mistakes, big ones and small ones. There's nothing wrong with that since it is all part of being human. However, it's often overlooked that being human also means being magical. Even with our flaws and foibles, we rise. We can do better than survive if we choose to acknowledge the magic of a human just being. We can *thrive*.

If you can, I recommend you check out the sacred sites that are close to you. Even if you live nowhere near Niagara Falls, do some digging, and you might find bodies of water near you with magical, mystical lore that calls to you. It's one thing to hear about sacred sites and another thing entirely to actually be there. Can't find anywhere close to you? Never fear. Even the very moisture in your breath is sacred water. It's a part of you that you can't escape, and that's something to be deeply grateful for.

Water represents your hopes and dreams, your emotions, and the deepest truths you have of yourself. Work with water, and you will learn more about yourself than you have over the entire course of your life. You will find that water has an uncanny way of bringing you inspiration and transforming the negative into what you prefer like no other element can. You can use this element to foster a productive flow when you want to work, need a creative boost, or just want to enjoy the moment on your own or with those you love. You can use water's energy to find your true, divine destiny so that you can live purposefully every day.

I hope this book lights a fire in your heart so that you begin your magical journey with water. I also hope to help you realize that this resource is one that we need to be more mindful of as we use it. Just because everyone else is ruining the environment with scant regard for what's happening to water worldwide doesn't mean that you should too. Always recognize that just as water can and does help you, you should do the right thing and help it too.

Finally, please make water meditation a daily practice. There's nothing quite like it to boost your awareness of water's magical properties. You see, there's only so much you can learn from books and resources online. Some things you only learn through constant practice. The more you work with water, the more you'll get intuitive nudges about what stones, colors, days, times, and other correspondences belong to this element.

Consistent practice will make water magic more personal to you, and the more personal it is, the more powerful your spells and rituals will be. So, even if you have no reason to cast a spell or do a ritual, commit to meditating with this element rather than let weeks and months go by without mindfully interacting with water. The gifts it will bring you are tremendous and unending. How do I know for sure? You're going to have to find out for yourself.

Here's another book by Mari Silva that you might like

Your Free Gift (only available for a limited time)

Thanks for getting this book! If you want to learn more about various spirituality topics, then join Mari Silva's community and get a free guided meditation MP3 for awakening your third eye. This guided meditation mp3 is designed to open and strengthen ones third eye so you can experience a higher state of consciousness. Simply visit the link below the image to get started.

https://spiritualityspot.com/meditation

References

Alexander, Skye. Find Your Goddess. Avon, MA: Adams Media, 2018.

Bartlett, Sarah. The Key to Crystals: From Healing to Divination—Advice, and Exercises to Unlock Your Mystical Potential. Beverly, MA: Fair Winds Press, 2015.

Bedau, Mark A., and Carol E. Cleland. The Nature of Life: Classical and Contemporary Perspectives from Philosophy and Science. Cambridge: Cambridge University Press, 2010.

Bethard, Wayne. Lotions, Potions, and Deadly Elixirs: Frontier Medicine in America. Lanham, MD: Taylor Trade Publishers, 2004.

Blavatsky, H. P. The Secret Doctrine. London: The Theosophical Society, 1893.

Bradley, Ian. Water: A Spiritual History. London: Bloomsbury Publishing, 2012.

Budge, Sir Ernest Alfred Wallis. The Book of the Dead: Translation. London: Kegan Paul, Trench, Trubner & Co. Ltd., 1898.

Buxton, Richard. Imaginary Greece: The Contexts of Mythology. Cambridge: Cambridge University Press, 1994.

Dorsey, Lilith. The African-American Ritual Cookbook. Self-published, 1998.

Drewal, Henry John. Mami Wata: Arts for Water Spirits in Africa and Its Diaspora. Los Angeles: Fowler Museum at UCLA, 2008.

Eason, Cassandra. Fabulous Creatures, Mythical Monsters, and Animal Power Symbols: A Handbook. Westport, CT: Greenwood Press, 2007.

Liddell, H.G. & Scott, R. (1940). A Greek-English Lexicon. Revised and augmented throughout by Sir Henry Stuart Jones. With the assistance of. Roderick McKenzie. Oxford: Clarendon Press.

Newton, Michael. Hidden Animals: A Field Guide to Batsquatch, Chupacabra, and Other Elusive Creatures. Santa Barbara: Greenwood Press, 2009.

Soyinka, Wole. Myth, Literature, and the African World. Cambridge: Cambridge University Press, 1976.

Stein, Diane. Pendulums and the Light: Communication with the Goddess. Berkeley, CA: Crossing Press, 2004.

Verner, Gary R. Sacred Wells: A Study in the History, Meaning, and Mythology of Holy Wells & Waters. New York: Algora, 2009

Printed in Great Britain
by Amazon

21085854R00078